THE BEST
URBAN
HIKES:
BOULDER

Happy hiking!
Darcy

DARCY KITCHING

The Colorado Mountain Club Press
Golden, Colorado

The Best Urban Hikes: Boulder
© 2020 by Darcy Kitching

PUBLISHED BY

The Colorado Mountain Club Press
710 Tenth Street, Suite 200, Golden, Colorado 80401
303-996-2743   email: cmcpress@cmc.org
website: http://www.cmc.org

Founded in 1912, The Colorado Mountain Club is the largest outdoor recreation, education, and conservation organization in the Rocky Mountains. Look for our books at your local bookstore or outdoor retailer or online at www.cmcpress.org/.

CORRECTIONS: We greatly appreciate when readers alert us to errors or outdated information by contacting us at cmcpress@cmc.org.

   Darcy Kitching: photographer
   Takeshi Takahashi: designer
   Jodi Jennings: copyeditor
   Sarah Gorecki: proofreader
   Jeff Golden: publisher

COVER PHOTO: Darcy Kitching

DISTRIBUTED TO THE BOOK TRADE BY
Mountaineers Books, 1001 Klickitat Way, Suite 201, Seattle, WA 98134, 800-553-4453, www.mountaineersbooks.org

We gratefully acknowledge the financial support of the people of Colorado through the Scientific and Cultural Facilities District of greater metropolitan Denver for our publishing activities.

TOPOGRAPHIC MAPS created with CalTopo.com software.

WARNING: Although there has been an effort to make the trail descriptions in this book as accurate as possible, some discrepancies may exist between the text and the trails in the field. Hiking in the mountains involves some risks. This guidebook is not a substitute for your experience and common sense. The users of this guidebook assume full responsibility for their own safety. Weather, terrain conditions, and individual technical abilities must be considered before undertaking any of the routes in this guide.

Printed in Korea
ISBN 978-1-937052-54-6

CONTENTS

Sunrise on the Flatirons, viewed from NCAR Mesa.

Foreword

My husband calls me the Pied Piper of Boulder. It started in spring 2015, when I became a volunteer walking movement leader with the Walk2Connect Cooperative, an organization started in Denver by a friend of mine, Jonathon Stalls, who had walked across the United States. Inspired by Jonathon's mission to elevate our natural form of movement to a powerful tool for community development, I took on the creation of the Boulder Walk2Connect group, known locally as the Boulder Ramblers. Since then, more and more people have followed me and my passionate co-leaders and Walk2Connect colleagues all over Boulder County, joyfully exploring this beautiful place we get to call home.

Over the past four years, our Boulder Ramblers community has grown tenfold, from just over 100 to more than 1,500 people, with multiple weekly walks attracting up to 25 people at a time, and more for special events. We have trained dozens of leaders and developed a host of unique routes and invitations that attract people from around Boulder and beyond. It has been incredibly rewarding to see our group grow and to witness the development of new friendships, participate in major life events of community members, and celebrate all the ways walking has brought so many creative, caring, and curious people together.

Long before volunteering with Walk2Connect, I was already a dedicated walker, hiker, and urban explorer. I grew up hiking with my family in Colorado and spent my young adulthood in the Pacific Northwest, living an active everyday lifestyle and going on annual backpacking adventures. International travel, too, fostered my love of exploring places on foot. My passion for walkable cities eventually led me to pursue a master's degree in urban planning and community development, which

Boulder Ramblers on the South Boulder Creek Trail, an oasis of calm in the city.

gave me the tools to advocate for walkable everyday environments designed with and for the people who need them most.

My relationship to walking and hiking fundamentally changed when I became a mother in 2012. For the first time,

I directly experienced some of the challenges people with mobility issues face every day. Frustrated by places I couldn't push a stroller, I began to understand just how vital it is that we make wide, smooth sidewalks and pathways a priority for all. I also had to reframe my own ideas about what constitutes a good hike. With my son in tow, in his stroller or on my back, I had to slow down, be satisfied with shorter outings, and be willing to experience the beauty of our nearby natural areas through his eyes (which often meant stopping at the side of a stream for 30 minutes to splash and hunt for colorful rocks). I found that rather than heading for the hills, we often just wanted to go somewhere beautiful and convenient, with flat trails, restrooms, and places to play. Most of the urban hikes in this book honor the needs of parents, older adults, and people with mobility challenges, offering a variety of accessible routes you can complete in a couple hours or less.

This book would not have been possible without the faithful support of my family and my fellow Boulder Ramblers. I am forever grateful for the friendship, encouragement, and enthusiastic engagement of our remarkable community of urban hikers. Whether you are visiting Boulder or you live in the area, I hope you enjoy getting to know Boulder County's bounty of urban trail systems and nearby natural areas the way the Boulder Ramblers have.

Use this book to get outdoors, connect with nature, spend time with friends and family, and discover special new places to return to again and again. Happy urban hiking!

Introduction

This book highlights the scenic urban trail systems east of the foothills. Boulder County and the municipalities included here—Boulder, Lafayette, Longmont, Louisville, Niwot, and Superior—annually invest millions of dollars in developing and maintaining the extensive soft-surface and paved trail networks described in this book, making everyday hiking accessible and enjoyable year-round for everyone. The trails traverse open space areas, parks, and greenways; follow natural and human-designed waterways; and highlight the beauty of the Colorado Piedmont area.

BOULDER'S LONG HISTORY OF OPEN SPACE PRESERVATION

The preservation of open space for recreation, agricultural use, and wildlife habitat is a deeply held value in Boulder. As far back as 1898, City of Boulder residents passed bond measures to allow the city to purchase land for preservation, starting with the area around present-day Chautauqua Park, the site of the magnificent mountain backdrop pictured on this book's cover. In 1967, Boulder voters made history by approving the first sales tax in the nation dedicated to purchasing and preserving open space. That tax led to the development of the city's Open Space and Mountain Parks (OSMP) Department, which manages wildlands and agricultural leases on open space within the City of Boulder. As of 2019, OSMP manages 45,000 acres of land and 155 miles of trails throughout the city.

Recognizing the impact of rapid population growth on the wild and cultivated lands throughout Boulder County, the Boulder Board of County Commissioners created a Parks and Open Space Department in 1975. Since 1975, the county has preserved more than 100,000 acres of land for recreational and

Spring wildflowers on the Foothills Trail.

agricultural use. The county's dedication to land preservation set an example for the adjacent cities of Longmont, Lafayette, and Louisville, all of which now have voter-approved open space taxes for land acquisition and management.

HOW TO USE THIS BOOK

The beauty of urban hiking is that it requires no training and no special equipment, not even a backpack. As I recently over-heard a hiker on a Chautauqua trail say, "The goal of this is to be outside and chill." Just pick a trail and go!

The 22 trails in this book are located within a short drive of downtown Boulder, and many are accessible by bus. Each hike description includes a rating from easy to difficult. Most hikes are relatively flat, with minimal elevation gain.

Boulder County greenways follow irrigation ditches, like this one along the Coal Creek Trail.

- "Easy" hikes are less than five miles with no significant elevation gain.

- "Moderate" hikes are longer than five miles, or more strenuous.

- "Difficult" hikes involve noticeable elevation gain (over 800 feet).

The distance listed covers only the trail sections described. Most of the trails in this book link up to larger networks through neighborhoods and open space lands. As you get to know the trails, extend your explorations to surrounding areas and see how many you can connect!

The times listed are approximate, based roughly on walking a mile in 20 minutes, plus added time for increased difficulty. While rest stops are not factored into the time, there are scenic places where you might want to linger. Take your time and enjoy the gorgeous views from the trails.

SUGGESTIONS FOR THE BEST EXPERIENCE

Before embarking on an urban hike in Boulder, follow these trail tips for the best experience.

- **Check your route.** Always check to ensure a trail is open. Mud closures are common on some trails during wet weather, and livestock grazing and routine trail maintenance can close areas or trail sections at any time. Boulder County Open Space, the City of Boulder OSMP Department, and the City of Longmont Parks, Open Space and Trails all maintain updated interactive online maps indicating all closures.

- **Manage high altitude.** Boulder is 5,328 feet above sea level. If you have recently moved to the area or are visiting from sea level, start out on shorter, flat trails and gradually work up to the highest elevations. Always carry plenty of water, rest often, and wear sunscreen and a sun hat. The thinner air in Colorado allows UVA and UVB rays to penetrate skin more quickly than at sea level.

Be sure to check that your chosen trail is open before you go. See interactive maps on the websites for Boulder County, the City of Boulder Open Space and Mountain Parks, and the City of Longmont Parks and Trails.

Explore Boulder County's agricultural past and present on these hikes.

- **Pay attention to kids.** When hitting the trails with little ones, note the elevation gain, whether the hike is stroller-friendly, and whether bicycles are allowed if your kids would rather roll than walk. Help children follow trail etiquette by walking or riding bikes on the right side of the trail to make way for bicyclists approaching or passing from behind. Note that many of the trails in this book have restroom facilities at one or more locations, as well as benches for resting. The best trails for kids are the shorter ones with water, artworks, and play areas along the way. Amenities are noted in the trail descriptions.

- **Stay hydrated and comfortable.** Always carry water, even if you don't think you'll need it. Stay hydrated by drinking water before, during, and after your hike. Dress in breathable layers to stay comfortable in any weather. And especially on longer hikes, be sure to pack a windproof and waterproof outer layer, extra socks, and a hat.

- **Stay aware of wildlife.** Chirping and chattering prairie dogs will be your frequent companions along many hikes in this book, though they won't approach people or dogs. Rattlesnakes are also common in this area during the warmer months. Keep an eye on the trail ahead of you and maintain your distance if you see a snake. You are much more likely to encounter a non-venomous bull snake than a rattlesnake on these trails. Bull snakes look similar to rattlesnakes, but don't have rattles and aren't dangerous.

- **Stay aware of other trail users.** On multi-use trails stay on the right to avoid bicycles, and don't tune out with headphones.

Black-tailed prairie dogs live in colonies on Boulder's grasslands.

Boulder's urban hikes are spectacular in the fall.

- **Keep track of your location.** Many of the trails in this book are loops and return to your starting point. For trails that travel in one direction only, plan how to get back to the starting place before you go. If you don't want to walk back the way you came, carpool and leave one car at each end. You can use the Transit app or Google Maps to find bus connections, or plan to use a ride-sharing app to hail a ride when you reach the end of the hike.

- **Carry a smartphone.** It's a great idea to carry a smartphone with a map app to check your location if you get turned around, or to discover trail extensions. Download the Boulder Area Trails app for quick access to local maps and real-time trail status updates.

ADDITIONAL TOOLS

The Boulder Area Trails Coalition (BATCO) is a great resource for maps at www.bouldertrails.org. Several of the trails in this book are links in the Trail Around Boulder, a proposed 37-mile loop around the city, all on dirt, conceived by BATCO. The Trail Around Boulder is not yet complete (several segments through private property have not been approved or acquired), but you can find a map showing current and future links in the loop at www.trailaroundboulder.org.

The Boulder Ramblers are on the Walk2Connect Cooperative website, www.walk2connect.com, and on Facebook and Twitter, where you can share your photos and suggestions. Also check out Boulder Walks, the City of Boulder's walking program, at www.boulderwalks.org. Boulder Walks hosts urban hikes, including an annual 26-mile "Walk 360" loop around the city that is part of the city's June Walk and Bike Month festivities. Boulder Walks also hosts monthly walks highlighting the city's extensive pedestrian infrastructure network.

1. A Taste of Chautauqua: Bluebell Loop

TRAILHEAD	Chautauqua
RATING	Easy
DISTANCE	2.1 miles
TIME	1 hour
ELEVATION GAIN	502 feet
USAGE	Chautauqua Park trails are for hikers only. Most allow dogs on leash, or off leash with City of Boulder Voice and Sight tags (see bouldercolorado.gov/osmp/voice-and-sight). The dirt trails are rocky and uneven.
STROLLER FRIENDLY	No

COMMENT: Chautauqua Park is emblematic of everything that makes Boulder distinctive, from its magnificent mountain backdrop and massive Flatiron rock formations to its history of open space preservation, active outdoor rec-

The light on the Flatirons in Chautauqua Park is spectacular at sunrise.

Summer poppies bring pops of color to the Meadow Trail.

reation, and residents' passion for lifelong education and self-improvement. The Boulder Chautauqua, established as part of a nationwide movement of adult education summer camps in the late nineteenth century, spearheaded the city's preservation of wildlands in 1898. Today, Boulder's OSMP Department manages more than 150 miles of trails in designated natural areas around the city.

Be sure to stop at the Chautauqua Ranger Cottage to pick up trail maps and brochures, chat with rangers, learn about wildlife in the area, let kids explore activities, and use the restroom before your hike. Fill water bottles outside at the bottle-filling station behind the Ranger Cottage.

This hike offers a quick and easy introduction to the Chautauqua trail system. It meanders below the Flatirons for fantastic views, up through ponderosa pine forest to junctions with more challenging trails, around the southeast side of the park to a historic picnic shelter, and back to the Ranger Cottage.

Add your own cairn to the collection at the junction of the Bluebell and First/Second Flatirons Trails.

GETTING THERE: Chautauqua Park is located at Baseline Road and 9th Street in Boulder. Parking is free on weekdays and is $2.50 per hour on weekends from Memorial Day through Labor Day. Use the free Park to Park shuttle on summer weekends to get to the trails from downtown Boulder and other locations. Find more information about the shuttle route and parking at parktopark.org.

THE ROUTE: Starting from the back of the Ranger Cottage, turn right (away from the main Chautauqua Trail) and hike north toward Baseline Road. Two trails run parallel to Baseline: Meadow Trail and Baseline Trail. Turn left at the signpost onto the Meadow Trail, which cuts across the hillside above Baseline. This trail affords great views of the Flatirons to the left and wanders through beautiful fields of wildflowers in the spring and summer. At the first trail junction, stay to the left and join up with the Baseline Trail, heading west

The Bluebell Shelter, built in 1939.

toward Gregory Canyon. At the second trail junction, turn left to go up through the trees to the Bluebell-Baird Trail, heading south. Pass the Ski Jump Trail (site of an actual tow line and ski jump until the mid-1960s) and continue hiking due south on Bluebell-Baird. The rocky trail is moderately steep here.

At about 0.75 mile, you will reach a major trail junction, where the Chautauqua Trail, Bluebell-Baird Trail, and the trail to Flatirons Loop and the 1st and 2nd Flatiron Trail meet. For an added challenge (and 250 additional feet of elevation gain), go up the Flatirons Loop Trail, which returns to the Bluebell-Baird Trail on the southeast side. Otherwise, continue straight through the forest, staying on Bluebell-Baird. The trail evens out here across the front of the hills, then dips down a bit and meets the Bluebell Mesa Trail, which turns off to the left. Continue straight (southeast) on Bluebell-Baird.

The popular Chautauqua trails are quietest early in the morning.

At 1.3 miles, the trail reaches the historic stone Bluebell Shelter, built by the local Lions Club in 1923 and reinforced by the Civilian Conservation Corps in the 1940s. It's the perfect place for a picnic lunch. Restrooms are available 100 yards downhill at the junction of Mesa Trail and Bluebell Road. To continue the hike, turn left behind the picnic shelter and follow the Bluebell Spur Trail northeast (you can also walk down Bluebell Road, but the Bluebell Spur Trail offers more scenic views and tree cover). From Bluebell Spur, look out over the red roofs of the University of Colorado campus to the northeast and take in the view of the city. The trail curves around to the west and joins up with the main Chautauqua Trail. Turn right and follow Chautauqua Trail back to the Ranger Cottage and the parking area.

A TASTE OF CHAUTAUQUA: BLUEBELL LOOP

N

Gregory

0.4mi

Baseline 0.2mi

0.1mi

0.1mi

0.1mi

1.0mi

0.1mi

Klondike

Sumac

TRAILHEAD

Gregory Canyon

0.1mi

0.3mi Meadow

0.1mi

0.1mi

0.1mi

0.1mi

0.1mi

0.2mi

Ski Jump 0.2mi

0.1mi

First Pinnacle
Second Pinnacle

0.1mi

0.1mi

Flatironette

0.3mi Chautauqua Trail

0.3mi

0.3mi

Bluebell Baird Trail

ALTERNATE OPTION

Third 0.1mi

0.1mi

0.1mi

Bluebell Mesa

0.1mi

0.3mi

0.3mi

The Spy

0.2mi

0.1mi

ALTERNATE OPTION

0.4mi

McClintock Trail

First Flatiron

Flatironette

0.2mi

0.1mi

0.1mi

0.2mi

0.2mi

0.1mi

Third Flatironette

0   0.1   0.2   0.3   0.4 miles

0.1mi

2. Lovin' on Boulder: Heart-Shaped Loop

TRAILHEAD	22nd Street and King Avenue
RATING	Moderate
DISTANCE	4.0 miles
TIME	2.5 hours
ELEVATION GAIN	750 feet
USAGE	This route primarily uses dirt trails, with one section of concrete path and a short section on a residential street. Bicycles are not permitted on the dirt trails referenced here but may be present on the street section. Dogs are not allowed on the Upper McClintock Trail at any time.
STROLLER FRIENDLY	No

COMMENT: In the 1950s, the U.S. Department of Commerce chose Boulder as the ideal home for a new scientific research campus focused on radio communications and the development of standardized measurement tools. Today, the National Oceanic and Atmospheric Administration (NOAA), the National Telecommunications and Information Administration (NTIA), and the National Institute of Standards and Technology (NIST) all maintain research and development

Fall color on the Skunk Canyon Trail.

Skunk Canyon scenery is worth turning around for!

labs at the federal campus on Broadway and 27th Street. This urban hike takes you alongside the labs to the spectacular City of Boulder OSMP trails just northwest of the campus and over to a little-known lookout with great views of the city and the foothills. Enjoy exploring the Skunk Canyon, Enchanted Mesa, and Upper and Lower McClintock Trails, where dense ponderosa pine forests, lush expanses of meadows, spectacular mountain and city vistas, and an alluring tree tunnel will leave you lovin' on Boulder for a long time! This hike is particularly beautiful in late spring and early summer, when the wildflowers are in bloom and the forests are spectacularly green.

Restrooms are available at Chautauqua Park, halfway along the route (though this route does not take hikers directly into the park, you can exit the McClintock Trail at mile 2.75 to use the amenities, if needed).

GETTING THERE: This hike starts at the entrance to the U.S. Department of Commerce campus at the junction of King Avenue and 22nd Street in Boulder. From Broadway, turn west onto Baseline Road and south (left) onto 22nd Street, following it to the end. Park along 22nd or King Avenue. The SKIP bus runs frequently down Broadway and is a great option for getting to this hike. Get off at the Baseline stop, then walk west on Mariposa Avenue or Bluebell Avenue to 22nd and walk south to where the street ends at King.

THE ROUTE: Start by walking through the open side of the black metal gate at the end of King Avenue. The U.S. Department of Commerce campus is open to hikers, and the public is welcome to use the sidewalk along the northwest edge of the campus. Once you are through the gate, turn right and follow the wide concrete sidewalk along the chain-link fence. You can peek into Green Mountain Cemetery on the right as you follow the fence. Among the notable Boulderites buried there are nuclear physicist and cosmologist George Gamow, artist Anne Ophelia Dowden, and poet Edward Dorn.

At the first path junction, turn right to continue following the sidewalk along the cemetery fence. On your left will be the Commerce Children's Center, the daycare facility for the campus. Continue along the sidewalk, cross the asphalt service road, and follow the sign for the Skunk Creek Multi-Use Path. The path curves around through some trees and crosses a bridge. Follow the Skunk Creek Path to the dirt social trail that turns off to the right. You will see a wooden post at the turn and a silver-colored metal gate with a stop sign on it at the far end of this social trail. Walk up to the gate and go around it on the left, entering onto the NIST service road. From this wide dirt road you can look straight ahead to the southwest, where the perfect triangular summit of Bear Peak rises in the distance. Just to the left of the mountain you can see Devil's Thumb, a prominent rock formation visible from around south Boulder.

The McClintock Trail "tree tunnel" is particularly beautiful in the spring and summer.

Walk up the service road to the first hairpin turn (at about 0.8 mile), then turn left onto the Skunk Canyon Trail. Look for the trail sign just past a wire fence off the service road. This trail can get muddy after snow and rain; the OSMP Department has reinforced the trail in several places with wooden planks. Follow the Skunk Canyon Trail, keeping to the right at every trail junction all the way up to Kohler Mesa. The trail makes long switchbacks up the open hillside, which features sumac bushes that turn from green to bright red in the fall.

You will walk past two junctions: the trail to NCAR Road, and the continuation of Skunk Canyon Trail. At the second junction, take the Skunk Canyon Spur up the hill on the right. As you reach the top of the hill, you will enter a ponderosa pine forest. Take a moment to look back toward Bear Peak and take in the sweeping view of scenic Skunk Canyon.

On Kohler Mesa, look for the trail signpost with two arrows pointing to the Kohler Mesa Trail; take the left path. At about 1.6 miles, you will reach a T in the trail, where the signpost shows two arrows pointing left toward the Mesa Trail; go right. You will quickly reach another junction; follow the left fork here, toward Enchanted Mesa. When you reach the wide, well-traveled Enchanted Mesa Trail, which looks like a four-way intersection, walk straight across it and keep heading northwest on the connector trail. The trail narrows and almost looks like a social trail, but it is an established connector trail. The next T junction is the Mesa Trail. Turn right and follow the Mesa Trail straight (northwest) down the hill to McClintock Trail. Look for the trail sign on the right and make a sharp right onto McClintock, which heads northeast.

The Upper McClintock Trail is densely forested and offers a unique sense of being surrounded by trees and bushes in an otherwise mostly open area. You can periodically look through the trees on the left to capture good photos of the First Flatiron. Hike down the hill past a set of log stairs leading right (the McClintock Spur Trail). Continue to the left down to where the Upper McClintock Trail intersects the Enchanted Mesa Trail. You will see a stone bridge that crosses a small creek on the left. Stay right of the bridge and enter the Lower McClintock Trail through the trees, just slightly to the right of where you left the upper trail.

Continue hiking on Lower McClintock, keeping right past a trail junction at about 2.75 miles that is marked by a large boulder and a small log fence. Hike down through the enchanting tree tunnel alongside a narrow creek, past the wooden stairs to the left; these lead up to 12th Street

The "snag" at the top of Four Pines Trail, with the red roofs of the University of Colorado campus on the horizon.

and the historic Chautauqua Auditorium. Walk past a huge granite boulder on the left to the trail's end at Bellevue Drive. Turn right and walk up Bellevue. This street section does not have a sidewalk, so watch for cars and walk on the left side of the street toward traffic for maximum visibility and safety. Keep right at the intersection with King Avenue, continuing to walk on Bellevue. Keep left at the next intersection with Mesa Canyon Drive and take the sidewalk that begins on the left, following Bellevue as it curves around to the northeast. Turn right onto Sierra Drive and walk up the hill to the end of Sierra, which terminates at the Four Pines Trail.

Hike onto the Four Pines Trail and go up the open hill to the top, where two pine trees and a sandstone bench invite a rest. From here, you can look out over the red tile-roofed buildings on the University of Colorado campus to the northeast, and

Wildflowers abound on the Four Pines Trail in the spring and summer.

you can see Mount Sanitas and the foothills farther north, to the left. The Green Mountain Cemetery is visible downhill to the southeast. Hike down the hill on the trail past a large snag—a dead tree left to provide habitat for wildlife. The trail has been reinforced to prevent hillside erosion, but it can still get very muddy in wet conditions.

Exit the Four Pines Trail onto King Avenue and turn right. Walk down the street to end where you started. Check out the well-stocked Little Free Library on the south side of the street along the way!

TRAILHEAD

3. Sawhill Ponds and Walden Ponds Wander

TRAILHEAD	Heatherwood Trailhead at 75th Street
RATING	Easy
DISTANCE	4.0 miles
TIME	1.5 hours
ELEVATION GAIN	62 feet
USAGE	The soft-surface trails referenced in this route are primarily for hikers only, with a short section of multi-use trail. Dogs are allowed on leash only.
STROLLER FRIENDLY	Yes, for jogging/all-terrain models

COMMENT: Boulder County and the City of Boulder maintain two adjacent properties, both former gravel quarries transformed by nature and preservation into wetland wildlife habitats in east Boulder. The Walden Ponds Wildlife Habitat was named for Boulder County Commissioner Walden

The Heatherwood Trail parallels Boulder Creek on the approach to Walden Ponds.

The City of Boulder Water Resource Recovery Facility is visible across Cottonwood Marsh.

"Wally" Toevs, who spearheaded the campaign to turn the gravel pits into a wildlife preserve in the 1970s. The habitat consists of five ponds, several multi-use paths, and a pedestrian-only interpretive boardwalk on the northern half of the property. The Sawhill Ponds area to the south, managed by the City of Boulder, is for hikers only, with a path around the perimeter of the wetland habitat. The properties are linked at three points along the southern edge of Walden Ponds Trail and the western edge of Duck Pond. This hike is rewarding year-round, with lush greens in the summer, vibrant fall colors, and quiet beauty in the winter with views through the trees to the mountains beyond. Vault toilets are available near the east end of the boardwalk on the Boulder County property and at the Walden Ponds Trailhead.

GETTING THERE: This route starts at the Heatherwood Trailhead west of 75th Street just south of Jay Road. From central Boulder, take Arapahoe Road east to 75th, then turn left (north) and drive to the small parking area on the west side of the road, past the signs to Walden Ponds and just past the City of Boulder Water Resource Recovery Facility.

THE ROUTE: The Heatherwood Trail starts on the west side of the trailhead parking lot. Make a left onto the trail and walk under the power lines toward Boulder Creek. The trail follows alongside the creek through a lush cottonwood forest, then turns south to follow the fence next to the City of Boulder's Water Resource Recovery Facility. Look to the right across the pond for a beautiful view of the mountains. At the southwest corner of the wastewater treatment plant, the trail branches to the west and south; turn right to walk west along the northern edge of Bass Pond and the Ricky Weiser Wetland. The Walden Ponds property borders private farmland, and you can often see cows grazing on the other side of the fence as you follow the trail. Enjoy the pastoral calm of this quiet place, and consider bringing a pair of binoculars for bird watching.

Follow the trail as it curves to the south along the western edge of the Ricky Weiser Wetland. You will come to a fence and a small gate at the border between Walden Ponds and Sawhill Ponds. Walk through the gate onto the Sawhill Ponds property and turn right. Follow the perimeter trail to the southwest as it wanders between a series of small ponds. The trees thicken here and provide welcome shade in the summer. Stay on the wide multi-use path as it curves to

Walking around Walden and Sawhill Ponds is rewarding any time of year.

Boulder's Bear Peak, Green Mountain, and the Flatirons are clearly visible from Walden Ponds.

the east just north of another pond. This area features large cottonwood trees, native grasses, and typical marshland plants like cattails, and offers beautiful views through the trees to the mountains beyond.

Walk east to the next trail junction, then turn left (north) and walk between two small ponds. Follow the trail to the northeast alongside a large pond, continuing north to the border with Walden Ponds. Walk through the gate and jog right to head north on the trail toward a small pond (Duck Pond) on the right, where an interpretive sign and a red stone bench invite a rest. To your left, you will notice the small green house that houses the Boulder County Volunteer Naturalist Program archives, which is not accessible to the public. To your right, there is a road and a narrower trail just north of the road. You can turn right onto the trail and walk alongside the cattails to the boardwalk. The boardwalk features two viewing areas over Cottonwood Marsh, where it is common to see great blue herons, ducks, and other wetland birds. In the summer, the cattails are green and

Explore the boardwalk at Walden Ponds to learn about the area, watch birds, and rest on built-in benches.

lush, providing beautiful habitat for butterflies. During fall, the dense reeds invite red-winged blackbirds and other songbirds whose plumage stands out against the earth tones of the marsh. Continue walking east to the end of the boardwalk to find a picnic shelter and restrooms.

Boulder County provides printed copies of a comprehensive field checklist of more than 100 different bird species that frequent the Walden Ponds and Sawhill Ponds area, which you can pick up at the trail map kiosk near the Walden Ponds parking area east of the boardwalk, just past the restrooms. You can also download a PDF of the guide, along with other field guides and checklists, from the Boulder County website, at www.bouldercounty.org/open-space/education/field-guides-and-brochures/.

Walk back west along the boardwalk and check out the excellent interpretive signs that tell the natural and human-influenced history of the area. Turn right at the trail along the western edge of Cottonwood Marsh and head north toward the wastewater treatment facility. Join the Heatherwood Trail and walk back north/northeast to the parking lot.

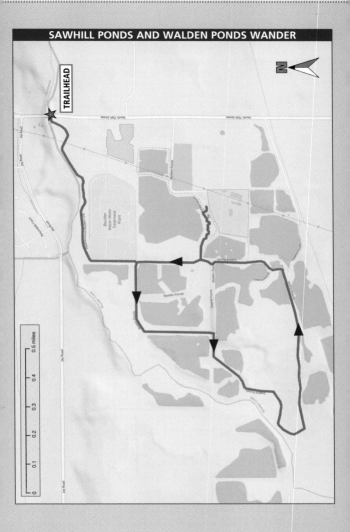

SAWHILL PONDS AND WALDEN PONDS WANDER

TRAILHEAD

N

Boulder Waste Water Treatment Plant

Walden Ponds

0   0.1   0.2   0.3   0.4   0.5 miles

4. Teller Farm and White Rocks Ramble

TRAILHEAD	South Teller Farm
RATING	Moderate
DISTANCE	5.0 miles (one way)
TIME	2 hours one way/4 hours round-trip
ELEVATION GAIN	166 feet
USAGE	The Teller Farm and East Boulder Trails are soft-surface multi-use trails open to hikers, bicyclists, and equestrians. Dogs are allowed on leash on the section south of Valmont Road only. No dogs are allowed on the trails north of Valmont Road.
STROLLER FRIENDLY	Yes, on the South Teller Farm Trail; no, on the North Teller Farm and East Boulder Trails

COMMENT: East Boulder's scenic rolling hills, ponds, irrigation ditches, and agricultural lands tell a moving story about human settlement and nature's resilience. The Teller Farm area was once part of the town of Valmont and has been continually farmed for more than a century. The ponds in this area were once gravel quarries, supplying stone for road projects. Today, nature has reclaimed the gravel pits as cattail-rimmed wetlands with abundant wildlife, and the White Rocks Nature Preserve provides sheltered habitat for bald eagles and other nesting birds. The irrigation ditches still provide valuable water for crops and ranch land, and mining has shifted to oil and gas extraction. The route described here is 5.0 miles long from the South Teller Farm Trailhead to the White Rocks Trailhead on 95th Street. Hike both directions for a four-hour adventure, carpool and park a car at either end, or use a ride-sharing app to get picked up at

The Teller Farm Trail offers sweeping views of the mountains all year round.

95th Street. Restrooms are available at the South Teller Farm Trailhead only.

GETTING THERE: The South Teller Farm Trailhead is north of Arapahoe Road between 75th and 95th Streets. From downtown Boulder, drive east on Arapahoe and look for the brown trailhead sign on the left past 75th Street. Turn onto the dirt road leading north to the parking area. The JUMP bus stops at the road to the trailhead on Arapahoe.

THE ROUTE: The trail starts at the northeast corner of the South Teller Farm parking lot. Go through the gate and turn right, walking east on the wide, soft-surface trail. Turn left onto the East Boulder Trail at the first junction with Teller Lake and follow the trail northeast as it winds alongside a

A few small oil and gas extraction pads are located along the Teller Farm and White Rocks Trails.

Water rights and mineral rights are equally complicated in Colorado, and this hike in eastern Boulder County provides a perspective on both. Farmers began diverting water from the six natural streams in Boulder Valley as early as 1859. They used teams of oxen or horses to cut deep trenches in the earth with plows or V-shaped tools called "ditchers." Farmers had to claim their water rights quickly and register their ditches, or they would lose seniority to those who beat them to the county clerk's office. Today, more than 150 privately owned irrigation ditches and reservoirs provide water to farms, ranches, and homes throughout Boulder County. Rights to the water flowing through the ditches belong to shareholders in the various ditch companies, but the surrounding land is typically owned by others. Ditch companies are granted prescriptive easements to maintain the facilities, which can be a surprise to landowners who might not know about an easement when they purchase the property. Similarly, the mineral rights to drill for oil and gas can be severed from the surface property or leased to a third party. When this happens, oil and gas drilling can happen even if a landowner does not want drilling on the site. Boulder County does not recognize oil and gas development as a permitted use of open space lands and will not voluntarily agree to lease or sell the mineral rights on its properties to oil and gas developers. But where the mineral rights already belonged to others before the land became open space, the county has little recourse to prevent drilling. Boulder County continues to work with state lawmakers and mineral rights holders to minimize the impact of oil and gas development on open space lands.

neighborhood on one side and farmland on the other. Take in the view of majestic Longs Peak to the west. At the northern edge of the neighborhood, the trail follows the historic Leyner Cottonwood Number 1 Ditch, which irrigates the farmland in this area. Cross the bridge over the ditch and walk along the stand of cottonwood trees that line a fence. In the summer, the cottonwood trees provide plenty of shade before noon. In the fall, abundant milkweed pods along the trail split open and send their wispy seeds out on the wind.

At about 2.0 miles, walk past a small oil and gas extraction site and go through the fence leading to the North Teller Farm Trailhead on Valmont Road. Go through another gate past a hay storage area on the left and walk past the trail map kiosk. Walk through the trailhead parking lot (there are no restroom facilities here) to the northwest corner and continue walking on the trail that parallels Valmont Road.

The historic site of Valmont, Colorado, viewed from the White Rocks Trail.

Cross Valmont at the marked crosswalk. Join the White Rocks Trail north of Valmont (remember that dogs are not allowed on this section). Walk past the historic Teller farmhouse and barn, through lush, protected wetlands along the ditch. Cross an abandoned rail line and follow the trail along the eastern edge of a large pond. Look for raptors and great blue herons here.

At 3.25 miles, cross the bridge over Boulder Creek and continue north toward White Rocks. Two farm roads intersect 0.25 mile north of the bridge. Cross the next bridge over an irrigation ditch and stay on the trail to the right of the blue gate. The trail goes up a hill and parallels the road for a short distance, turning into a narrow dirt track. Watch out for mountain bikers here. The White Rocks formation and nature preserve lie beyond the fences and are not accessible

Rolls of hay with Bear Peak in the background, near White Rocks.

THE BEST URBAN HIKES: BOULDER

Looking west from the White Rocks Trail near the trailhead at 95th Street.

to the public, but OSMP rangers occasionally offer geology and wildlife tours of the area (learn more at bouldercolorado .gov/osmp).

The trail leads onto a broad, sweeping mesa, with fantastic 360-degree views of the area. Walk north and cross a private, paved farm road, then turn right at the trail junction and walk east to the White Rocks Trailhead. The trail, which is rutted and rough on this section, passes a neighborhood on the left, with a natural ditch and the private road off to the right. It ends at 95th Street. Either turn around and hike back or catch a ride back to the South Teller Farm Trailhead.

TRAILHEAD

5. Boulder Valley Ranch Choose Your Own Adventure Loops

TRAILHEAD	Left Hand or Boulder Valley Ranch
RATING	Moderate
DISTANCE	10.7 miles total from Left Hand Trailhead; 5.0 miles from Boulder Valley Ranch Trailhead
TIME	2–4 hours
ELEVATION GAIN	520 feet total
USAGE	The Left Hand and Boulder Valley Ranch Trails are dirt and gravel multi-use trails open to hikers, bicyclists, and equestrians. Dogs are allowed on leash. Note that the Left Hand Trail is prone to mud closures in wet weather.
STROLLER FRIENDLY	No, on the Left Hand Trail; yes, on the Sage and Eagle Trails

COMMENT: The area east of Highway 36 between Boulder and Lyons has long served as ranch land for settlers who raised cattle and sheep. Remnants of historic homesteads and an ore smelter can be found in the area, and the City of Boulder still leases much of the Boulder Valley Ranch land for agricultural use. The rolling grasslands and bluffs are beautiful places to explore on foot, featuring sage and low bushes in the north, and cottonwoods and willows along Farmers Ditch in the south. This hike offers varied terrain and wide-open views of the foothills and Flatirons, Haystack Mountain, and north Boulder. Choose your own adventure on this easily accessed urban hike, going the whole distance of 10.7 miles or cutting that in half by starting at the first loop. Be aware that rattlesnakes are common in this area in the summer. Restrooms are available along the Left Hand Trail and at the Boulder Valley Ranch Trailhead.

Prairie dogs greet hikers on the Left Hand Trail.

GETTING THERE: To start at Left Hand Trailhead, take Highway 36 (Foothills Highway) from Boulder or Lyons to Neva Road and drive east to the trailhead, which is on the south side of the street just west of North 39th Street. The Left Hand parking area is larger than the lot at Boulder Valley Ranch and is typically less busy. To start at Boulder Valley Ranch Trailhead, take Highway 36 to Longhorn Road and drive east to where the public road ends at the trailhead. Parking is free at both trailheads.

THE ROUTE: Starting at Left Hand Trailhead, go through the gate and past the trail map kiosk, walking west on Left Hand Trail. The dirt single-track trail takes you through a prairie dog colony past a Boulder County-managed picnic shelter and restroom. The trail curves east toward Left Hand Valley Reservoir, which is fenced off from the trail. Pass through several agriculture gates and over a few small wooden footbridges along the way, heading south toward Boulder Valley Ranch. Look for red-winged blackbirds, magpies, and red-tailed hawks as you follow the rising and falling landscape.

From this northern approach, the trail takes you directly toward Green Mountain and Bear Peak in the distance, and you can see Devil's Thumb on the left flank of South Boulder Peak.

Be aware of potential mountain bikers along the narrow single-track and step off the trail to let them pass, if necessary. At about 2.5 miles, cross a paved driveway and walk past two large elk sculptures on the left. The Boulder Valley Ranch Trailhead is directly ahead, about 2.8 miles south of the Left Hand Trailhead. Turn left in front of the gate to continue onto the Sage Trail, heading east (or, if starting at Boulder Valley Ranch, walk to the gate north of the parking lot, go through it, and turn right).

The Sage Trail is a wide, crushed-gravel, multi-use trail. Walk on the right side to let bicyclists pass on the left. Follow the wide-open Sage Trail clockwise around Boulder Valley Ranch, past a working horse ranch on the right. The trail goes up a gentle rise and meets the Eagle Trail on the northeast side of the loop. Stay to the right and go down the hill onto Eagle Trail, walking toward the small pond to the south. Around the pond is a verdant wetland area with cattails, willows, and

The Boulder Valley Ranch landscape includes a small pond and wetland.

abundant birds. Pass the pond and walk southwest toward the cottonwood trees along Farmers Ditch on the southern side of the property. The trail curves around to the west through a beautiful area well shaded by cottonwoods.

At the next trail junction, turn left up the rocky hill to stay on Eagle Trail (or, for a shorter hike, stay on Sage to close the first loop and return to the parking area). From the top of the mesa, pause to look south toward Boulder. Walk toward the small, red-roofed metal shade structure on the other side of a fence. Go through the fence and turn left onto the Mesa Reservoir Trail (note that dogs are not allowed on this trail). Hike clockwise around Mesa Reservoir for a small loop that affords 360-degree views of Boulder and the foothills to the south, Boulder Reservoir to the east, and Haystack Mountain, the only conical geological feature on the landscape, to the northeast. On the southern edge of Mesa Reservoir, go through a gate and stay on the Mesa Reservoir Trail to

Cottonwood trees lining Farmers Ditch provide shade and beautiful scenery.

The 360-degree view from the top of the mesa overlooking Boulder Valley Ranch features Haystack Mountain to the northeast.

the right (avoid the Hidden Valley Trail to the left, which borders a shooting range).

Follow the trail down the hill behind Mesa Reservoir, and at the next four-way trail junction, turn right onto Degge Trail. Walk through a gate and head back

It's EASY to share the trail! The City of Boulder offers great guidelines for all trails where hikers, bicyclists, and equestrians may meet.

toward the reservoir up a short rise. At the top of the hill, head southeast to rejoin Eagle Trail at the shade structure. Go back through the gate and take the rocky connector trail back down to the Sage Trail. Turn left and close the loop by walking to the Boulder Valley Ranch Trailhead. End there or walk through the gate and head north on Left Hand Trail to return to the parking area 2.8 miles to the north.

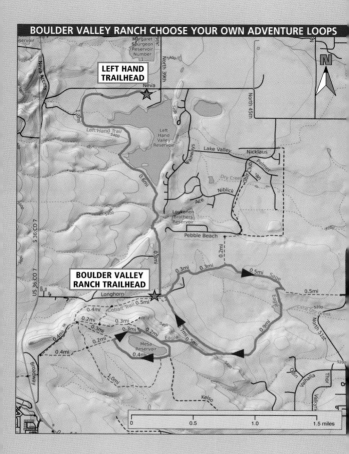

6. Two Loops on the Foothills Trail: Hogback Ridge and Old Kiln

TRAILHEAD	Foothills
RATING	Difficult
DISTANCE	4.5 miles
TIME	2 hours
ELEVATION GAIN	859 feet
USAGE	The Foothills Trail, which connects the two loops described here, is a wide, soft-surface multi-use trail, allowing hikers, bicyclists, and equestrians. Dogs are allowed on leash. The rocky Hogback Ridge Trail is open to hikers only, no dogs or bikes allowed. The Old Kiln Trail is a narrow dirt trail open to hikers only (no bikes) and dogs on leash.
STROLLER FRIENDLY	No

COMMENT: Get loopy in North Boulder! Just 0.3 mile from Broadway, the Foothills Trail is easily reached by bus, bike, or on foot, offering avid urban hikers a quick and easy way to experience Boulder's mountain beauty. Follow this trail to Hogback Ridge, a challenging 800-foot climb above the Dakota Ridge neighborhood, and the most vertical hike in this guide. Hogback Ridge is quieter and more accessible than popular Mount Sanitas, with spectacular, sweeping views of the Boulder peaks and the city below. If you're visiting from sea level, be sure to try some of the lower hikes first to acclimate to the city's elevation. After tackling Hogback Ridge, hike over to the easy Old Kiln Trail for a soothing cooldown alongside a flowing stream. Together, these two loops offer a great perspective on Boulder's topography and geology and provide an entry point to the extensive OSMP trail system. No facilities are available at the trailhead, and shade is scarce in this area, so be sure to pack plenty of water, snacks, and sunscreen, and use the restroom before you hit the trail.

GETTING THERE: Park at the Fourmile Canyon Creek Trailhead, located on the south side of Lee Hill Drive 0.3 mile west of Broadway, just past 6th Street. Look for the pedestrian crossing with the flashing lights. To get there by bus, take the SKIP to the Lee Hill Drive stop and walk west to the trailhead.

THE ROUTE: From the parking lot, cross Lee Hill Drive at the pedestrian signal and head north on the packed-gravel Foothills Trail, which parallels 5th Street into the Dakota Ridge neighborhood. The trail turns west along Dakota Boulevard, then curves north again at a trail map kiosk. Take the Foothills North Trail north to the Hogback Ridge Trail connector, located just over 0.5 mile from the parking lot, and turn left. Head counterclockwise up the loop, taking the trail to the right where the loop begins shortly after the connection with Foothills North Trail.

Hogback Ridge rises above Boulder's Dakota Ridge neighborhood, where deer graze in the meadow.

The "hogback" formation at the top of the ridge is composed of Dakota Sandstone laid down during the Cretaceous period and uplifted over millions of years.

The trail becomes steep, rocky, and narrow as you head north up the ridge; stop and look behind you for spectacular views of Green Mountain, the Flatirons, and Bear Peak, as well as north Boulder and the eastern plains below. A few ponderosa pines dot the savannah landscape here, and the lichen-covered Dakota Sandstone boulders become larger as you near the top of the ridge. The trail turns west for a short climb to the top. At the top of Hogback Ridge, the trail goes behind the boulders that line the summit (forming the "hogback" outcropping, reminiscent of a razorback hog, hence its name). Scramble up over the rocks for great views of the city. There is plenty of room to sit and relax at the top. Follow the trail behind the boulders and down a set of stone steps to the steep descent along the southeast side of the loop. The bare hillside is reinforced with log steps along the southern edge of the trail.

Follow the trail back down to the connection with Foothills North and turn right. Walk back to Lee Hill Drive and cross at the pedestrian signal. Go through the Fourmile Canyon Creek parking lot to the opening in the log fence at the southern edge of the lot (walk toward Bear Peak, the tallest mountain in the distance). At the trail sign kiosk, walk to the right onto the Foothills South Trail. If water is flowing in the creek, cross using the large stepping stones. This area was severely affected by the 2013 floods that brought rocks and debris rushing down Boulder Creek and

Stepping stones help hikers cross a shallow creek to access the Foothills South Trail.

Find the Old Kiln that gives this trail its name on the north side of the second loop.

its tributaries and created massive erosion on many Boulder trails. The city's OSMP Department completed repairs to the trail in 2017, and it now provides easy access to the trail system south of Lee Hill Drive.

Hike past the first connection to the Old Kiln Trail on your right and follow the trail to the southwest corner of the black chain-link fence around the off-leash dog park on your left. Look for a bench straight ahead—and, on sunny days, a paraglider or two—and turn right onto the Old Kiln Trail here, beside two short wooden fences. Follow the trail along the gentle rise to the northwest. Stay to the right at the junction with the Old Kiln Spur Trail at the top of the hill and continue on Old Kiln down around to the north. The trail takes you to a sandy creek bed, where rocks of various sizes have been deposited by floodwaters. As the trail turns east along the creek, look to the right to see the old Lee Hill Lime Kiln constructed into the hill. Unusual deposits of limestone

Paragliders can often be seen sailing over the Foothills Trail.

in this area provided lime for early construction projects, perhaps even for some buildings on the University of Colorado campus. The flash flooding in September 2013 washed away much of the hillside here and lowered the ground level, so the historic kiln structure has been reinforced with lumber to prevent its erosion.

Hike past the kiln, following the trail along the creek bed to the southeast. You will pass a sandy beach area on the right before reconnecting with the grassy savannah and the Foothills Trail. Turn left on the Foothills Trail and head back north toward Lee Hill Drive and the parking lot.

7. Wonderland Lake Loop

TRAILHEAD	Wonderland Lake
RATING	Easy
DISTANCE	1.6 miles
TIME	30 minutes
ELEVATION GAIN	87 feet
USAGE	The trail around Wonderland Lake is a wide, soft-surface multi-use trail open to hikers, bicyclists, and equestrians. It is one of the most accessible trails in the OSMP system and is easy to navigate with a stroller or sport wheelchair. Dogs are allowed on leash.
STROLLER FRIENDLY	Yes

COMMENT: Wonderland Lake is a wonderful place to enjoy a quiet retreat right in the city. It is ideal for families with young children and is a popular place to take kids fishing. The lake provides protected habitat for wetland creatures, including a variety of ducks and geese, and is ringed with cattails and other wetland plants. Fishing is allowed only in

Wonderland Lake provides a peaceful oasis in the city.

Ducks dabble on the lake early in the morning.

designated places, including the peninsula just south of the start of the loop trail. At less than 2.0 miles, the loop trail around the lake is easy to navigate. There is a playground and picnic shelter at about the half-mile mark, on the south side of the lake, which provide a reward and respite for little hikers and their families. No restroom facilities are available on this trail.

GETTING THERE: The address of the Wonderland Lake parking lot and trailhead is 4201 Broadway, Boulder. The parking lot is on the west side of Broadway. It is accessible by the SKIP bus, which runs frequently along Broadway.

THE ROUTE: The trail starts on the west side of the parking lot, just to the left of the Foothills Nature Center building (not open to the public except during special OSMP programs). Walk west toward the lake and the foothills on the connector trail. The loop trail begins near the lakeshore; step down the three stairs to the left where the trail branches, or, if you're using a stroller or wheelchair, go a little farther to take the

The south shore of the lake is a protected wetland habitat for birds and other wildlife.

ramped trail down toward the water. At about 0.25 mile, a peninsula extends off to the right through the trees. It is a favorite spot for fishing and letting kids play along the shore.

Hike clockwise around the lake, following the dirt trail south along the eastern edge of the water. The trail sits atop an earthen dam with the lake down to the right and a floodplain to the left. Enjoy watching ducks on the water. At the southeast edge of the water, the dirt trail ends at a concrete path. Turn right to follow the lake, taking the concrete path along

Wildflowers line the trail on the west side of Wonderland Lake, blooming through early summer.

Wonderland Lake offers an easy and scenic urban hike.

the edge of the neighborhood, with the wetland extending down to your right. Stay to the right and cross the bridge across a concrete spillway. If you're hiking with little ones, stop and enjoy the playground just beyond the bridge. Otherwise, continue walking on the concrete path along the water.

Rejoin the dirt trail at about the 1.5-mile mark at the trail map kiosk and the wooden fence near the lake to the right. Follow the dirt trail along the western edge of the lake and stay to the right at the junction with the Foothills Trail. Take the trail back around to the east and walk to where the trail crosses the Silver Lake Ditch. At this point, the trail parallels a private asphalt road on the right and leads to Utica Avenue. Turn right on the sidewalk and walk for a short way along the right side of the street. The reentry to the Wonderland Lake Trail is just past the "Speed Hump" sign. Turn right onto the dirt trail, then left to continue closing the loop. At the junction with the connector trail, continue to the left and walk back to the parking lot.

WONDERLAND LAKE LOOP

TRAILHEAD

8. Flatirons Vista Loop

TRAILHEAD	Flatirons Vista
RATING	Easy
DISTANCE	3.5 miles
TIME	1.5 hours
ELEVATION GAIN	280 feet
USAGE	This is a multi-use dirt trail accessible to hikers, bicyclists, and equestrians. The trail is wide enough to accommodate all users. Dogs are allowed on leash. Stay alert for bicyclists and horses and walk on the right.
STROLLER FRIENDLY	Yes, for jogging/all-terrain models only

COMMENT: Don't judge a trail by its trailhead! Flatirons Vista is the southernmost trail in Boulder County, and the rolling prairie at the border of Boulder and Jefferson Counties can look a little barren. But the peacefully quiet open space and stunning views of Boulder's iconic Flatirons from just

Sunrise and sunset are great times to enjoy the majestic views from the Flatirons Vista Trail.

Sit and watch the light change on the Flatirons from the top of the mesa, overlooking the Doudy Draw area.

west of the trailhead off Highway 93 offer reward aplenty for enthusiastic urban hikers. Do this hike on its own or connect along the way with the Doudy Draw Trail and explore more loops near scenic Eldorado Canyon. Ponderosa pine forests and sweeping views of the canyon, South Boulder Peak, and Bear Peak make this hike a fantastic foray into all south Boulder has to offer. It is particularly beautiful during the early morning and late evening hours, when hawks sail over the trees and the sun catches the Flatirons at interesting angles. This area is occasionally used for livestock grazing. Be aware of potential agriculture closures in the fall. Restrooms are available at the trailhead.

GETTING THERE: The Flatirons Vista Trailhead is located on Highway 93 (Foothills Highway/Broadway) just south of the light at the junction with Highway 128 (West 120th Ave). The trailhead and parking lot are on the west side of the highway. This is a parking fee area: parking is free for vehicles registered in Boulder County and is $5 for all others.

THE ROUTE: Start at the west side of the Flatirons Vista parking lot, near the trail map kiosk and toilets. Take the Flatirons Vista North Trail on the right. Pass the connector trail to Greenbelt Plateau and head west toward the mountains. Stay to the right at the junction with Flatirons Vista South Trail; go up the hill on Flatirons Vista North.

At the top of the hill, about 0.5 mile from the trailhead, cross under the power lines and take in the first clear view of the Flatirons. This is the magnificent vista that gives the trail its name. Also visible are the National Center for Atmospheric Research (NCAR) to the northwest on the horizon, and South Boulder Peak with the saddle to Bear Peak farther west. You can see the burned trees standing like bristles on the saddle between South Boulder and Bear Peaks, a result of the 2012 fire that burned the back side of Bear Peak. Ponderosa pine

Wind turbines at the National Wind Technology Center are visible from several points along the trail.

trees dot the prairie here as you head toward the mountains. To your left, on the southeast horizon, you can also see the giant wind turbines being tested at the National Wind Technology Center, which is part of the National Renewable Energy Laboratory (NREL) Flatirons Campus.

Hike due west to the junction with the Doudy Draw Trail. Where the two sets of power lines meet, cross the small cow grate or go through the gate and turn left onto Flatirons Vista South. (Don't take the left path that leads directly under

The west side of the Flatirons Vista trail offers a relaxing forest immersion experience.

Flatirons Vista offers a clear view of the saddle between South Boulder Peak and Bear Peak.

power lines due south. Before you head south, take in the view at the fence, looking out onto the Boulder peaks and the striking Eldorado Canyon. Flatirons Vista South takes you through a dense ponderosa pine forest, with lots of places to stop and take in the views along the way. This trail is less busy and popular than trails closer to Boulder, making it a great place to pause and breathe in the forest's natural phytoncides, chemicals emitted by the pine trees that both protect the plants and help decrease stress in humans.

The trail continues southwest through the forest, then curves around to the east along the county line fence. Cross the junction with the path that leads from the north under the power lines and stay to the right. Continue east into the open prairie and stay on Flatirons Vista South, going downhill. To the south, on the horizon, notice the NREL wind turbines and the Arcosa Lightweight aggregate production facility, just over the border in Jefferson County. As you follow the trail, you will pass a small pond on the left. Go around the pond to the north, and at the junction with the Prairie Vista Trail, take it straight on to the parking lot, rather than turning left to stay on Flatirons Vista South. The parking lot is just 0.2 mile east of this junction.

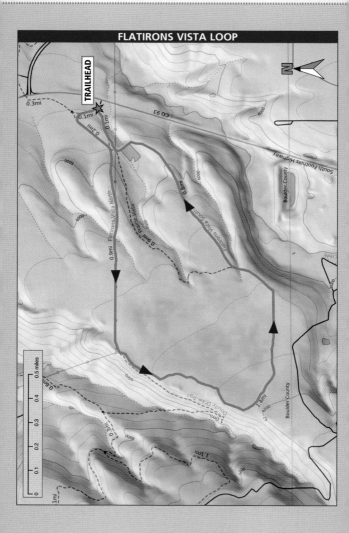

FLATIRONS VISTA LOOP

TRAILHEAD

N

0.3mi

0.1mi

0.2mi

0.1mi

CO 93

South Foothills Highway

Boulder County

6000

6000

6000

Flatirons Vista North

0.9mi

Flatirons Vista South

0.9mi

0.8mi

6000

Doudy Draw Trail

0.6mi

1.0mi

1.1mi

1.0mi

1.1mi

0.3mi

1mi

6000

6000

6000

6000

6000

Boulder County

0 0.1 0.2 0.3 0.4 0.5 miles

9. NCAR to Woods Quarry Out and Back

TRAILHEAD	NCAR
RATING	Moderate (two steep hills)
DISTANCE	3.7 miles
TIME	2 hours
ELEVATION GAIN	739 feet
USAGE	The OSMP hiking trails around NCAR are open to hikers only. Dogs are allowed on leash or off leash with City of Boulder Voice and Sight tags (see bouldercolorado .gov/osmp/voice-and-sight for information).
STROLLER FRIENDLY	No

COMMENT: The National Center for Atmospheric Research (NCAR) Mesa Laboratory building was designed by architect I. M. Pei in 1963 and quickly became one of Boulder's

Sunrise on NCAR Mesa is spectacular.

NCAR is a Boulder icon, visible from around south Boulder and beyond.

most iconic structures. Perched atop Table Mesa in south Boulder, the NCAR Mesa Laboratory embodies a kind of contextual modernism. It stands as a stylized version of the natural sandstone features surrounding the building—a unique blend of human ingenuity and geological elegance. The free NCAR Visitor Center is open every day of the week and is a fantastic place to start a hike. Go inside to check out interactive weather exhibits, see the original scale model of the building, fill water bottles, and use the restroom before exploring the area trails. NCAR even has a café open for breakfast and lunch on weekdays.

This urban hike connects NCAR with Woods Quarry, another site of historical significance for the city of Boulder. In the 1890s, Jonas Bergheim and Frank Wood quarried sandstone slabs from the mountainside southwest of Table Mesa for use in building sidewalks and structures in Boulder. The impractically located quarry closed sometime before 1920, and the City of Boulder bought the site to prevent further development and preserve the land for recreational use. Today Woods Quarry offers hikers a fun place to sit back and relax on sandstone slabs arranged into chairs, while taking in spectacular views of the eastern plains.

GETTING THERE: NCAR's Mesa Laboratory is located at 1850 Table Mesa Drive. Drive up to the parking lot on top of the mesa, then park and walk to the visitor center or trailhead.

THE ROUTE: From the parking lot, the NCAR Trailhead is to the right of the building. Walk past the trail map kiosk onto the Walter Orr Roberts Trail and check out the interpretive signs about weather. Follow the signs to Mesa Trail on the western edge of the mesa. At the interpretive sign about snow turn left and drop down behind the mesa onto a rocky trail that leads to a saddle. From the saddle, you can

The Roosa Cabin is nestled in the woods near the Woods Quarry Trail.

Parts of the Mesa Trail near Woods Quarry have been paved with flagstones to prevent erosion.

Relax at Woods Quarry on a sandstone "sofa" built by previous visitors.

see Table Mesa Drive to the right. Go left up the stair steps to the top of the hill where you will see a large green water tank. Walk around the left side of the water tank, following the signs to Mesa Trail.

Continue on the NCAR Trail, heading west through ponderosa pines and following signs to Mesa Trail. Stop to enjoy the spectacular view of Devil's Thumb, Bear Peak, and the colorful meadow on the west side of the mesa. Take the right (north) fork at the next trail junction, heading down a single-track dirt trail to the Mesa Trail, with its distinctive red clay soil. Turn right and follow Mesa Trail down the hill to the bridge over a small creek bed. Go up the hill on the other side and hike northwest to the junction with Skunk Canyon Trail. Stay to the left on Mesa Trail. Walk through a densely forested area before the trail opens up again under the sandstone quarry. You can see scraps of sandstone slabs above and below the trail. The trail bends to the northeast and meets the Kohler Mesa Trail. Stay to the left and turn left onto Woods Quarry Trail just past the junction with Kohler Mesa. Look for the small stone Roosa Cabin in the woods nearby. The cabin was occupied as recently as the 1970s, but its provenance remains mysterious.

At the 1.5-mile mark, go up the log stairs built into the trail, which is the steepest section of this hike. Turn left and walk into the quarry area. Take a break to enjoy the views from a sandstone chair! From here, you can see NCAR, South Boulder Road extending off to the east, Valmont Reservoir, and more. When you're ready, retrace your steps to head back to the trail, but turn left instead of right, heading north on the gently sloped trail through the trees. This is the northern part of the Woods Quarry Trail, which forms a loop from the Mesa Trail. Follow the trail as it curves around to the right. You will reach a four-way trail junction. Turn right onto the Mesa Trail and walk south. You will pass the Roosa Cabin on the right and the junction with Woods Quarry and Kohler Mesa Trails. Continue south on Mesa, the way you came, toward NCAR.

Stay to the right past Skunk Canyon Trail, heading down to the creek and across the bridge, then continue past the trail you originally took from NCAR. Walk to the four-way junction with the Mallory Cave Trail, where you will see a trail map kiosk. Turn left to take NCAR Trail up the mesa to the water tank. From the water tank, stay to the right and follow the stair steps down directly east of the tank. It is easy to accidentally turn left and walk down the wide access road. Don't do that, or you will have to walk up NCAR Road/Table Mesa to get back to the parking area!

Follow the trail down to the saddle and up the back side of the mesa, returning to the Walter Orr Roberts Trail and the NCAR Trailhead.

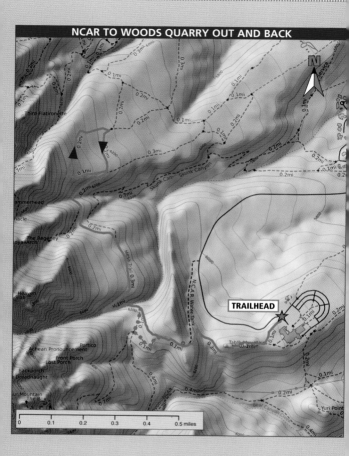

10. South Boulder Creek to Bobolink Out and Back

TRAILHEAD	South Boulder Creek on Marshall Road
RATING	Easy
DISTANCE	3.3 miles (one way)
TIME	1–2 hours
ELEVATION GAIN	10 feet
USAGE	The South Boulder Creek Trail is a mostly soft-surface, packed-gravel trail with a few sections of concrete path. Hikers, bicyclists, and equestrians are allowed. Dogs are NOT allowed on the first section of this trail, between Marshall Road and South Boulder Road.
STROLLER FRIENDLY	Yes

COMMENT: The South Boulder Creek Trail offers the perfect place for an early morning or late afternoon urban hike, as a warm-up for bigger adventures or just a relaxing wander along the water. This wide, flat trail is ideal for those walking with strollers or with a little one on a bike. From south to north, the South Boulder Creek Trail traverses active agricultural areas and connects to the East Boulder Recreation Center, ending at the beautiful Bobolink Trailhead, a popular place for nature play and picnics. Along the way, enjoy the shade of cottonwood trees, the chirping of birds and prairie dogs, and the occasional "moo" from grazing cows. This trail provides a great vantage point, too, on Boulder County's agricultural history, with several historic barns and sheds still standing in the fields. No facilities are available at the trailheads, but the East Boulder Recreation Center is a good place to stop to use the restroom, fill water bottles, and grab a snack, if needed.

The scenic South Boulder Creek Trail is especially lush and green in the summer.

GETTING THERE: This route starts at the trailhead on Marshall Road, just east of Highway 93 (Broadway). From downtown Boulder, take Broadway south past the traffic light at Greenbriar Boulevard and turn left at the first left-turn refuge past the place where Highway 93 bends to the south. Turn right at the stop sign onto Marshall Road and park along the road. To get there by bus, take the SKIP from central Boulder down Broadway to the first stop after the bus turns onto Greenbriar Boulevard. Walk north on Greenbriar to Broadway, cross at the traffic light, walk down the steps on the north side of the intersection, turn right and follow the wide concrete path southeast to Marshall Road. The trailhead is on the east side of Marshall Road.

THE ROUTE: The trail begins at the gate on Marshall Road just south of the short connector road from Broadway. Go through the gate and head east on the trail. This is a popular place for bicyclists, so be sure to walk on the right side of the path and stay aware of other trail users around you. The trail crosses the narrow Bear Creek Ditch and the Dry Creek Ditch, then winds past a lively prairie dog colony. Where the trail bends around to the north, a short boardwalk shores up the trail over the bordering wetland. The trail continues northeast along South Boulder Creek. Through trees to the left, past the fence separating City of Boulder property from University of Colorado property, you can see the CU South Trail.

At about 1.4 miles, go through the gate on the other side of the agricultural lease area and stay to the right along the paved US 36 Bikeway, going north under the highway bridge.

Historic barns add character to the landscape along South Boulder Creek.

Walk on the dirt path next to the pavement here, as this is a busy bikeway. On the north side of the underpass, stay to the right and go through another gate onto the soft-surface trail that continues north. Notice the old barn on the left and the spectacular view of the Flatirons, especially early in the morning. This is a great spot for an iconic Boulder photo. On the north side of the field, go through another gate and turn right on the path, then walk over the wide bridge over South Boulder Creek.

Walk due east to the next place the trail splits, at South Boulder Road. Head left through the underpass. On the north side of South Boulder Road, follow the path as it winds left and crosses two ditches, then bends to the right (north) again along the creek. At about 2.75 miles, stop to admire the large downed cottonwood tree along the creek, just before the side trail to the East Boulder Recreation Center. Through

The picturesque "snag" just south of the path to the East Boulder Recreation Center offers a fun photo op.

The pedestrian-only path near the Bobolink Trailhead offers a delightfully calming experience.

South Boulder Creek at Bobolink is a popular place for nature play among families with young children.

the curve of the tree, you can see the National Center for Atmospheric Research (NCAR) on its mesa just below Bear Peak. This is another spot for a classic Boulder photo.

Walk past the next trail junction, unless you want to take a break at the recreation center, at the end of the path to the left, and follow the soft-surface trail across the paved path. This last section of the South Boulder Creek Trail, which travels along the creek, is for pedestrians only, and provides beautiful shade, with several places to stop and rest next to the water. This is a favorite area for families with young children. There are several access points to the water, and sandy banks provide pleasant places to linger. Continue walking north to the Bobolink Trailhead. Turn around and head back from there or catch a ride back to the starting place.

TRAILHEAD

| 0 | 0.5 | 1.0 | 1.5 miles |

11. Twin Lakes Figure 8

TRAILHEAD	South Orchard Creek Circle
RATING	Easy
DISTANCE	4.0 miles
TIME	1.5 hours
ELEVATION GAIN	69 feet
USAGE	The Willows Trail west of Twin Lakes is a paved and soft-surface multi-use trail that allows walkers, bicyclists, and dogs on leash. The trails around Twin Lakes (managed by Boulder County) are soft-surface multi-use trails that allow walkers, bicyclists, and dogs on leash (east side) and off leash (west side).
STROLLER FRIENDLY	Yes

COMMENT: Gunbarrel's Twin Lakes Open Space offers a dog's paradise and is a delightful destination for an easy urban hike. The lakes are irrigation reservoirs filled from Boulder Creek and maintained by the Boulder and Left Hand Irrigation Company on behalf of shareholders who operate farms in the area. The amount of water in the lakes fluctuates throughout the seasons depending on demand, and the wetland supports a variety of wildlife and many mature cottonwood trees. It's a popular recreation area. Hikers with dogs will love the trail around the West Lake, where furry friends can roam freely off leash. The area around West Lake is enclosed by wooden fences with gates at four points around the lake. The connected trail around East Lake requires that dogs stay on leash and offers spectacular views of the Front Range. This route approaches the lakes from the west, following the Boulder and Left Hand Ditch through scenic deciduous forests rich with wildlife and opportunities for nature connection all year round. There is a port-a-potty at the Eaton Park Trailhead at Nautilus Drive on the north side of the lakes, as well as a small picnic shelter. Trash cans are provided at several locations for dog waste.

GETTING THERE: This hike begins on South Orchard Creek Circle, 0.2 mile west of Spine Road and just south of Orchard Creek Lane. From Boulder, take Foothills Parkway or the Diagonal Highway north to Jay Road. Turn right on Jay, then left on Spine Road. Turn left onto South Orchard Creek Circle, follow the street around to the north and park along the street. The trail begins on the east side of the street where the ditch flows through the neighborhood. Starting here allows for on-street parking, which is not allowed on Spine Road. From Longmont, take the Diagonal Highway to Spine Road, then turn south onto Spine and left onto South Orchard Creek Circle. The trailhead is also accessible by bus on weekdays: the RTD 205T bus runs down Spine Road and stops at Orchard Creek Circle/Wellington Road. If you take the bus, begin the hike from Spine Road.

The Willows Trail leading to Twin Lakes follows the Boulder and Left Hand Ditch.

Nature-inspired artwork lines the 63rd Street underpass.

THE ROUTE: Starting on the east side of South Orchard Creek Circle, begin walking on the paved path alongside the Boulder and Left Hand Ditch. The trail takes you through a quiet neighborhood, where you are likely to see rabbits, squirrels, and songbirds. At Spine Road, make a slight left to cross at the marked crosswalk, then rejoin the trail alongside the ditch. East of Spine Road, this trail is called the Willows Trail and is maintained by Boulder County. It is surrounded by mature cottonwood trees and offers a beautiful journey through lush urban forest.

At the next street, Wellington Road, cross with caution (it is a quiet street with no marked crosswalk) and turn left, walking a short distance to join up with the trail on the south side of Gunbarrel Commons Park, a private neighborhood park. Continue walking east on the crushed-gravel trail. Give yourself plenty of time to enjoy the light through the trees and the sounds of running water and birds. Cross another quiet street, Robinson Place, at grade, and continue walking east toward 63rd Street. Follow the trail through the underpass under 63rd, inside of which local artists have painted murals depicting the natural environment. East of 63rd Street, the trail joins up with the Boulder and Whiterock Ditch, paralleling both ditches to Twin Lakes.

The mountains of the Indian Peaks Wilderness are visible to the west.

At 1.0 mile, just east of 63rd Street, turn left where the trail splits and a blue and white sign points to Longmont and the LoBo Trail (see hike 15). Cross the bridge and head northeast, away from the houses and toward a more industrial-looking area. The trail enters a meadow; to its north you can see the fence around West Lake. Turn left at the next trail junction, heading due north. Keep to the left to reach the gate leading into the fenced West Lake Dog Park area. Go through the gate, turn left, and cross the wooden bridge. Dogs are allowed off leash here.

To hike a figure-8 around Twin Lakes, walk clockwise around West Lake and counterclockwise around East Lake. First, walk three-quarters of the way around West Lake, passing the gate and bridge at the northeast edge of the lake to continue hiking southeast along the earthen dam between the lakes. This area provides a comfortable sense of enclosure, almost reminiscent of a botanical garden. Enjoy the shade of the trees and stop to rest at any of the benches along the way.

Follow the path around the edge of West Lake to the fence on the southeast side. Go through the next gate and turn left, walking northeast along the Twin Lakes Trail. Cross the bridge, then turn immediately left toward East Lake. Cross the Boulder and Left Hand Ditch (take a peek through the trees to the left to see some of the water-management machinery), then turn right to follow the southeast side of East Lake. Walk counterclockwise around East Lake, enjoying the shade of the cottonwood forest. The path opens up on the northeast edge of East Lake, offering beautiful views of Longs Peak and the Indian Peaks to the west.

Hike around the northern edge of East Lake to the Eaton Park Trailhead at the end of Nautilus Drive. There is a BMX bike track to the right, a picnic shelter, and a portable toilet here. Just left of the trail map kiosk, turn to walk over the wooden bridge and go through the gate to the West Lake trail. Turn left to walk back along the earthen dam between

The enclosed area around West Lake is an off-leash dog park and a great place to hike.

Fall color graces the Twin Lakes area.

For a special end to this urban hike, head north on Spine Road just 0.1 mile to Sleepytime Drive and visit the Celestial Seasonings tea factory and café. Started in 1969 by Mo Siegel, Celestial Seasonings launched the specialty herbal tea industry, selling creative blends of chamomile, peppermint, hibiscus, and other herbs and spices with whimsical names in artistic boxes. At the Celestial Seasonings factory, you can enjoy free samples of the company's newest brews, shop for delicious teas and tea accessories, take a free factory tour, get a bite to eat, and learn about the history of this artful Boulder institution. Check celestialseasonings.com for hours and more details.

the lakes. Follow the trail around to the southwest corner of West Lake, to the first gate you entered. Go through the gate and head due south along the Twin Lakes Trail. Cross the bridge and turn right, heading toward 63rd Street. Follow the Willows Trail west along the ditch back to your starting place on Spine Road or South Orchard Creek Circle.

TWIN LAKES FIGURE 8

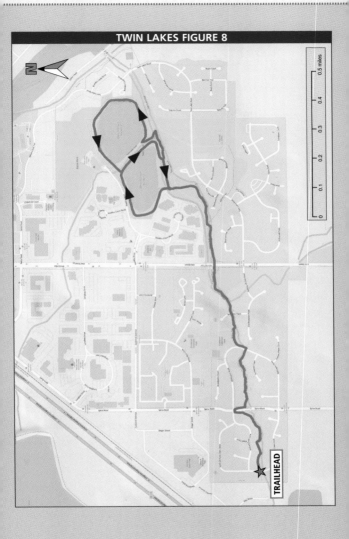

TRAILHEAD

0.5 miles

0.4

0.3

0.2

0.1

0

N

12. Linking Three Cities on the Coal Creek Trail

TRAILHEAD	Public Road
RATING	Moderate
DISTANCE	6.0 miles (one way)
TIME	2.5 hours one way/5 hours both ways
ELEVATION GAIN	358 feet
USAGE	The Coal Creek Regional Trail is primarily soft-surface with a few paved sections. It is a multi-use trail, allowing hikers and bicyclists. Dogs are allowed on leash.
STROLLER FRIENDLY	Yes

COMMENT: The Coal Creek Regional Trail was developed through the collaboration of Boulder County and four municipalities: Lafayette, Louisville, Superior, and Erie. It forms an active commuter corridor, inviting residents to walk or bike between work and home, and provides a quiet

A sculptural seating area on the Lafayette section of the Coal Creek Trail.

and relaxing recreational area for residents and visitors alike. Interpretive signs along the way tell the story of historic coal mining in the area, the people involved in developing the trail, and natural points of interest. The full length of the Coal Creek Trail, spanning the distance between Superior and Erie, is 14 miles. The 6.0-mile section described here connects the Public Road Trailhead in Lafayette with Grasso Park in Superior, traveling through Louisville along the way. Walk both ways to get more miles in, leave a car at either end, or use a ride-sharing app to catch a ride back to the starting place. Restrooms are available at the Public Road Trailhead, at Louisville Community Park, and at Superior Town Hall (during regular business hours) at the end of the route.

GETTING THERE: The Public Road Trailhead parking lot and restrooms are on the west side of South Public Road, 0.5 mile south of the intersection of South Boulder Road and Public Road. From Boulder, head east on Arapahoe Road for about 9.0 miles. Turn right (south) on Highway 287, then turn left on South Public Road. The small parking lot will be on your left just before Old Laramie Trail East (turn into the narrow driveway before the traffic light). You can also take the JUMP bus down Arapahoe to downtown Lafayette. Get off at South Boulder Road at Miner's Drive and walk south for 0.5 mile to join the Coal Creek Trail just east of Public Road.

THE ROUTE: The Public Road Trailhead in Lafayette offers well-maintained restrooms, a picnic table, benches, and a trail map kiosk. Arrive early in the morning to watch the mountains light up with the sun as you head west on the Coal Creek Trail, or try this hike on a cool evening and watch the shadows lengthen across the plains. From the parking lot, turn right (west) on the concrete path, which quickly transitions to a wide, soft-surface gravel trail through cottonwood trees along Coal Creek. Take care to walk on the right side of the trail to make room for bicyclists to pass. Throughout

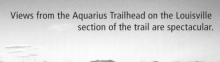
Views from the Aquarius Trailhead on the Louisville section of the trail are spectacular.

your hike, keep an eye out for the blue and white Coal Creek Regional Trail signs posted at main trail junctions and along neighborhood connections.

Take a moment to stop and read the interpretive sign about the Vulcan Mine and the fascinating history of coal mining in Lafayette at 0.3 mile. Farther on, as you approach Highway 287, turn left to stay on the Coal Creek Trail and follow the concrete path under the highway. On the other side of the highway, stay on the main path heading due west along the water. Soon, you will come to a series of interpretive signs spread over about a half-mile length of the trail, which feature detailed information about the area's riparian habitat and how the ecosystem functions. There are also benches and bench-sized boulders situated periodically along the trail, making it an inviting place to rest and listen to birds and the water flowing by. At 1.5 miles, cross over a wide bridge and turn left at the sculptural rock and metal sitting area, heading south toward the creek.

Just before you cross over the water, notice the sign on the right honoring JoAnn Dufty, a professional artist and the first Coal Creek/Rock Creek Trail coordinator in the 1990s, when the system was first established. It was visionaries like Dufty who were responsible for the development of the regional trails so loved by Boulder County residents today. Walk over the bridge and head up the hill toward the frontage road. Cross at the marked crosswalk and continue walking up the hill toward the Aquarius Trailhead. You are now in the city of Louisville!

At the top of the hill, stop to take in the spectacular view of the mountains in the distance and the farmland below. Longs Peak, the tallest mountain visible at more than 14,000 feet, is particularly stunning from this vantage point. Check out the "Peak Finder" sign to learn the names of all the mountain peaks you can see from the hill. The Aquarius Trailhead offers parking and a picnic shelter, but no other amenities. Follow the trail as it dips down the hill to the west and parallels Highway 42 (Empire Road) before going under it. Go through the underpass and turn right across the wooden bridge to stay on the Coal Creek Trail. Hike west along the road to the Courtesy Road underpass, rejoining the creek, and then walk under the railroad bridge.

The path curves north away from the water west of the railroad bridge. Just a few feet ahead, turn left at the Coal Creek Trail sign to cross County Road/Front Street at the crosswalk. On your right, across Bella Vista Drive, you will see Louisville Community Park. The park offers many amenities,

A historic barn sits across from Louisville Community Park.

including a summer splash pad for kids, a fenced-in dog park with a pond, rolling hills, restrooms, play structures, and a picnic pavilion. It's a great place to take a break, and it marks the halfway point of this hike. If you desire a more substantial break with lots of options for refreshments, cross the

Look for the blue Coal Creek Trail signs along the corridor to help you stay on the right trail.

park and walk north on Main Street into charming downtown Louisville.

The Coal Creek Trail parallels Bella Vista Drive for a short way, then turns left along Roosevelt Avenue and curves briefly to the right along Aspen Way. Notice the historic red barn on the left. The gravel trail turns to the left off Aspen Way and enters the Dutch Creek Open Space. Walk southwest toward the creek and the Coal Creek Golf Course. At the next four-way trail junction, turn left, heading south. A short way down the trail, you will see a blue sign cautioning hikers to look out for golf balls. At about the 4.0-mile mark, the trail turns due south toward a neighborhood. Go up the hill and cross Augusta Drive at the crosswalk. Here, the trail becomes a wide concrete sidewalk. Look for the blue and white Coal Creek Trail signs to guide your way through the neighborhood.

Augusta Drive meets St. Andrews Lane; cross St. Andrews Lane at the crosswalk and turn right, then cross St. Andrews Lane again a short way down the street, following the trail

The trail ends at Grasso Park in Superior, where the town's original wrought-iron jail cell is on display.

to the right toward the golf course. The trail briefly parallels West Dillon Road before curving around to the right and going under the road. Stop and enjoy a break at the golf course's public café (to the right on the other side of the parking lot just before the underpass) or continue through the West Dillon Road underpass. The paved trail gives way to gravel again as you walk toward Highway 36 (the Denver/ Boulder Turnpike), passing the City of Louisville's trail maintenance facility on the left and office buildings on the right. At Highway 36, the trail intersects with the US 36 Bikeway. Follow the concrete path straight on through the wide, well-lit underpass under the highway. On the other side, enter the Town of Superior. Notice the medical center on the left and the hotel on the right. Keep following the trail straight ahead, walking west along the creek.

In spring 2019, Superior completed its realignment of the Coal Creek Trail west of Highway 36. The new concrete trail curves along the creek behind new development, including restaurants and an event center. Finish this 6.0-mile hike by following the trail under McCaslin Boulevard to Grasso Park on the other side. Grasso Park, named for local coal miner and farmer Frank Grasso and his family, features historic buildings, farm machinery, and even the town's original jail cell! Enjoy a well-earned rest before walking back or catching a ride to where you started.

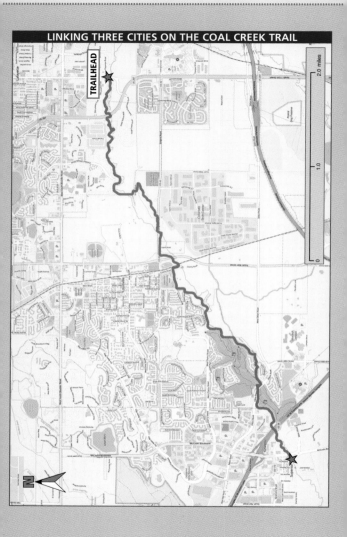

LINKING THREE CITIES ON THE COAL CREEK TRAIL

TRAILHEAD

2.0 miles

1.0

0

N

13. Rock Creek Ramble

TRAILHEAD	Carolyn Holmberg Preserve at Rock Creek Farm
RATING	Moderate
DISTANCE	6.1 miles (one way)
TIME	2.5 hours one way/5 hours both ways
ELEVATION GAIN	43 feet
USAGE	The Rock Creek Regional Trail is primarily soft-surface with some paved sections. Hikers, bicyclists, and equestrians are allowed. Dogs are allowed on leash.
STROLLER FRIENDLY	Yes

COMMENT: Rock Creek flows through southeast Boulder County, where coal mines tunneled underground a century ago and cattle still graze today. The mining and agricultural history of the county is well documented all along the Coal Creek and Rock Creek regional trail system, from Superior to Erie, with interpretive signs offering insights into past land uses and current wildlife inhabitants. The 6.0-mile segment

Stearns Lake at Carolyn Holmberg Preserve provides a picturesque start to this hike.

The wide-open nature of this trail affords panoramic views in all directions.

of the trail documented here connects Carolyn Holmberg Preserve (in what is technically Broomfield) and Flagg Park in Lafayette, on the eastern edge of Boulder County. Carolyn Holmberg was a director of Boulder County Parks and Open Space who helped facilitate the county's acquisition of land for ongoing agricultural and recreational use, historic preservation, and wildlife habitat.

The Rock Creek Trail links Boulder County's past, present, and future as it winds through active farmland and industrial areas. On this true urban hike, watch for birds of prey, enjoy breezes through the cottonwood trees along the creek, and experience the satisfaction of connecting the dots along this fascinating corridor, which forms a natural buffer between residential, commercial, and industrial areas. Restrooms are available at both trailheads on either end of this hike. Carpool with others and park a car at either end, walk both ways for a long urban hike, or use a ride-sharing app to get picked up at Flagg Park and return to your starting place.

GETTING THERE: Carolyn Holmberg Preserve at Rock Creek Farm is located off 104th Street south of West Dillon Road. From Boulder, take the Interlocken Loop/Northwest Parkway exit off Highway 36 and drive north to Dillon Road. Turn right, then right again on 104th. From Longmont or Lafayette, take Highway 287 south to Dillon Road and go west (follow the signs to the Northwest Parkway, but stay to the right to take Dillon) to 104th.

THE ROUTE: From the southeast side of the parking lot at Carolyn Holmberg Preserve, walk toward Stearns Lake and follow the trail on the south side of the lake. Pass the connection to the Cradleboard Trail on the right, continuing on around the lake. At the northeast edge of the lake, follow the trail to the right (east). At about 1.0 mile, pass the gate to the Rock Creek Farm; follow the small signs for the Rock Creek Trail. Farm roads cross the trail frequently here. In October, the farm is a vibrant and popular pumpkin patch.

Just after 1.5 miles, the dirt trail gives way to concrete and leads under Highway 287. Follow the trail to the right and under the highway. On the other side, the trail meets Rock

The Rock Creek Trail parallels an active freight rail corridor near the Lafayette medical center complex.

Creek. Cross the wooden bridge spanning the creek, then cross the train tracks at the pedestrian crossing indicated. Follow the signs to Flagg Park. At the next trail junction, stay to the left to take the trail connecting Superior and Lafayette; do not turn right toward Broomfield.

You will pass an industrial area on the left, then cross a small bridge over the creek. Cross Dillon Road at the cross-walk and follow the concrete path under the Northwest Parkway. Straight ahead, rejoin the gravel path and notice the medical center complex to the north. The trail takes you just to the east of the medical center, between train tracks on the left and Rock Creek and rolling fields to the right. The trail links to the medical center, offering an attractive outdoor connection for employees and visitors.

Just before the 4.0-mile mark, the trail winds between two industrial operations: a concrete company on the left, and a sand and gravel company on the right, with a school bus park-ing lot along 120th Street. Turn right where the trail meets 120th Street, walk along the sidewalk briefly, then follow the concrete path to the 120th Street underpass. On the east side of 120th Street, turn left and rejoin the soft-surface path

The approach to Flagg Park offers views of Mt. Meeker in the distance.

Watch out for holes in the trail made by resident prairie dogs!

northeast along the creek. The trail soon meets Horizon Avenue at a business park. Turn right and walk along the sidewalk briefly to the Horizon Avenue underpass. Alternatively, if the underpass is flooded, cross Horizon Avenue and walk to the left on the path next to the creek. The trail is well marked through this area. The dirt path leads behind the business park to the northeast and quickly reenters the prairie open space.

At almost 5.0 miles, the Rock Creek Trail merges with the Coal Creek Trail just before the confluence of the two creeks. Walk through the lively prairie dog colony and, if you like, take the side path on the left to the viewing area featuring two mounted interpretive signs. The signs relate the history of the development of the regional trail system, and the watersheds and wildlife in the area. Return to the main path and continue northeast. Cross a bridge and follow the gray packed-gravel trail. Notice a few small oil and gas extraction tanks in the area, and watch out for prairie dog holes in the trail!

The trail branches just before the 6.0-mile mark; follow the sign to Flagg Park to the left. Walk toward the creek and cottonwood trees. There is a picnic area on the bluff above the creek. Cross the bridge over the creek and walk to the parking area at Flagg Park. Restrooms are available here. Turn around and walk back for an all-day adventure, or catch a ride back from here.

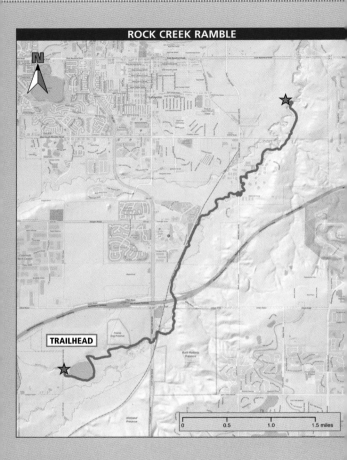

N

TRAILHEAD

| 0 | 0.5 | 1.0 | 1.5 miles |

14. Waneka Lake Loop

TRAILHEAD	Waneka Lake Park
RATING	Easy
DISTANCE	2.0 miles
TIME	45 minutes
ELEVATION GAIN	32 feet
USAGE	The trails around Waneka Lake are mostly soft-surface multi-use trails, with a short section of paved path on the east side. They allow walkers and bicyclists, and dogs are allowed on leash. The trails are wheelchair accessible. Fishing is allowed at different points around the lake.
STROLLER FRIENDLY	Yes

COMMENT: Lafayette's Waneka Lake Park, Greenlee Wildlife Preserve Open Space, and Thomas Open Space are all located just west of Highway 287 and downtown Lafayette. They

The Greenlee Wildlife Preserve on the north shore of the lake offers a boardwalk and a quiet space for bird watching.

offer a whole day's worth of attractions for families. In the summer, rent paddle boats or canoes from the Waneka Lake Boat House. Year-round, the area is ideal for bird watching, and the charming Isabelle Farm Store offers locally made crafts and food items. This is a favorite spot for local fitness groups to gather, and the City of Lafayette hosts bird talks on the afternoon of the first Sunday of each month at Greenlee Wildlife Preserve. Waneka Lake trails connect with pathways through the surrounding neighborhoods and Lafayette's Walk & Wheel Loop around the city center. Restrooms are available at the Waneka Lake Boat House and at the Isabelle Farm Store.

GETTING THERE: From South Boulder Road, take Ceres Drive to Caria Drive and park in the lot by the playground and boat house. From Highway 287, take West Emma Street due west to the parking lot on the east side of the lake. You can also access Waneka Lake through the Thomas Open Space off Baseline Road, by the Isabelle Farm Store. The 225 RTD bus travels down Baseline between Boulder and Lafayette on weekdays only.

THE ROUTE: Starting at Waneka Lake Park, walk left on the trail past the playground to travel clockwise around the lake.

Waneka Lake features a boathouse and great views of the Indian Peaks.

The trail around Waneka Lake provides open views on the southeast and shaded corridors on the northwest side.

Several picnic shelters, lots of trees, a Little Free Library, and attractive play equipment make this an ideal place for family outings. The lakeshore features cottonwood trees, cattails, and willow bushes. Pass the peace pole on the right and the basketball court on the left; continue around the lake to the right. Pass a trail connection on the left and look for the interpretive signs at the Greenlee Wildlife Preserve Open Space. Turn left to explore the wildlife viewing platform, pond, and lush wetland to the north. The path wanders around the wildlife preserve to the left and up to Baseline

"Surveying Our Future"—a sculpture by Geoffrey Newton Metalworks on Baseline, acknowledging the establishment of the 40th Parallel "baseline."

Road, but I suggest returning to the main path around Waneka Lake and heading left around the pond to walk north through the Thomas Open Space.

The trail on the east side of the Greenlee Wildlife Preserve takes you through the small working farm on the Thomas Open Space, past a horse barn on the left and gardens on the right. The City of Lafayette leases the land to Isabelle Farm, which grows root vegetables, salad greens, garlic, and other crops here. Walk to the charming Isabelle Farm Store on Baseline to pick up locally made goods and treats and to use the restroom, if desired. After exploring the north end of the Thomas Open Space along Baseline, turn back toward Waneka Lake and continue on the path to the left around the north and east side of the lake. Pass the parking area off

The Isabelle Farm Store is a great place to stop for refreshments on this hike.

The Isabelle Farm Store occupies a 3,200-square-foot barn at the entrance to Thomas Open Space off Baseline. The barn was built in 2012 by the City of Lafayette to provide a year-round retail and production center for the lessee of the 14-acre organic farm in the open space. Isabelle Farm has leased the land since 2007. The store is open every day from 10 a.m. to 6 p.m., all year round, with a two-week break in December. See www.isabellefarm.com for more information.

Emma Street and the adjacent Frisbee golf course. Look for the wooden sculpture of a great blue heron on a tree branch. Several benches are situated around the east side of the lake, offering fantastic views of the Indian Peaks in the distance.

Walk around the lake to the boat house, where restrooms are available, and back to the parking lot.

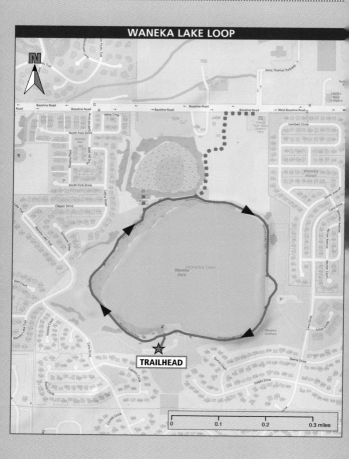

TRAILHEAD

15. Longmont to Niwot on the LoBo Trail

TRAILHEAD	Left Hand Creek at Longmont Recreation Center
RATING	Moderate
DISTANCE	5.6 miles (one way)
TIME	2 hours one way; 4 hours both ways
ELEVATION GAIN	141 feet
USAGE	This route uses concrete paths, sidewalks, and soft-surface multi-use trails. Dogs must be leashed on this route.
STROLLER FRIENDLY	Yes

COMMENT: Boulder County, the City of Longmont, and the City of Boulder collaborated to build the Longmont-to-Boulder (LoBo) Regional Trail beginning in 2003, and the

The LoBo Trail takes hikers through Left Hand Park, where art and amenities offer the ideal place to stop for a rest.

Look for the Tower of Compassion in Kanemoto Park.

trail system is still evolving. The current official trail comprises 12.0 miles of multi-use paths and on-street connections between Longmont and Boulder, linking trails through parks and open space, alongside rail lines, and under major streets. The route described here starts farther northeast than the LoBo Trail, beginning at the Longmont Recreation Center on Quail Avenue. Starting here affords hikers ample parking and transit connections, and the chance to fill water bottles and use the restrooms before hitting the trail. The City of Longmont's investments in everyday walking and hiking paths that link destinations with art and culture are evident. Look for the creative public art pieces and murals along the paths, enjoy the shade of cottonwood trees in the summer and the wide-open views in the winter, watch for freight trains going by, and make time to stop in the town of Niwot at the end of the hike to fully enjoy the adventure of connecting two cities by foot.

GETTING THERE: The address of the Longmont Recreation Center is 310 Quail Road. If you drive, go around the back of the recreation center to park in the north lot by the tennis courts. You can reach the recreation center by bus: take the LD 1/LD 2 bus from downtown Longmont, or the BOLT from Boulder.

THE ROUTE: The Left Hand Creek Trail begins on the northeast side of the tennis courts behind the Longmont Recreation Center. From the parking lot, follow the concrete path to the right of the tennis courts straight north. Turn left at the first junction, where the path curves to follow alongside Left Hand Creek. Go through the South Main Street underpass and continue along the creek to the southwest. Another underpass takes you under South Pratt Parkway. Look for the Longmont graffiti-style art on the west side of the underpass.

At about 1.0 mile, notice the five-story Tower of Compassion and the brass plaque on your right. The tower was commissioned by Jimmie and George Kanemoto in honor of their father, Goroku Kanemoto, and as thanks to the Longmont community for its support of their Japanese-American

Longmont graffiti-style art enlivens the underpass on the west side of Pratt Parkway.

family during WWII. Stop and read the plaque to learn about the symbolism of the tower, then continue walking on the concrete path between Left Hand Creek on the right and Missouri Avenue on the left. Look for the "Nature's Way" series of sculptures by Tim Watkins placed along this section, known as the Southmoor Park Greenway, including a mosaic fish water fountain, a "bat bench," colorful chairs, and a kinetic archway.

At 1.5 miles, take the Pike Road underpass and enter Left Hand Creek Park. There are restrooms and picnic shelters here, as well as two play areas and a whimsical sculpture of giant ants called "Picnic in Left Hand Park," by Robert Ressler. As you walk past the sculpted ants in the grass, look up to your right to spot several carved faces hidden high up on the trunks of the cottonwood trees along the creek. See how many you can find!

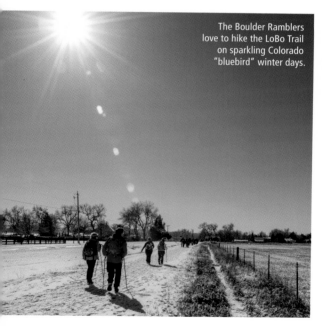

The Boulder Ramblers love to hike the LoBo Trail on sparkling Colorado "bluebird" winter days.

In the summer, ripe corn creates a green corridor along a section of the LoBo Trail.

The trail continues along Left Hand Creek to South Sunset Street. Turn right and take the marked crosswalk across the street, rejoining the path on the north side of the creek. The concrete path continues to South Hover Road. Take the Hover Road underpass and join the official LoBo Trail on the west side. Here, the path becomes a soft-surface trail. Stop to take in the great views of Longs Peak, with the cottonwood trees arching gracefully over the trail. The LoBo Trail soon curves to the southwest alongside an active BNSF Railway line. Watch for freight trains going past in the morning and evening (great photo opportunity!). At about 3.3 miles, a wooden bridge crosses over Left Hand Creek. Look for the creative ways the landowners shored up the creek banks in the past; old cars and trucks were embedded in the banks, which were exposed by erosion and flooding in the fall of 2013.

The land on the west side of Hover/95th Street is largely used for agriculture. The trail follows alongside broad fields and active ranch sites. Keep to the soft-surface trail to North 83rd Street, about 4.5 miles from the start. The trail turns

Turn off of the LoBo Trail at the Niwot Grange Park and walk over this bridge to end the hike in town.

due south and follows along the east side of 83rd for 0.2 mile. Cross over 83rd Street at the designated crosswalk and continue on the soft-surface trail on the west side of the street. The trail merges with a wide concrete sidewalk for 0.1 mile; after crossing Dry Creek Road, rejoin the soft-surface trail. Walk south along the trail for just over 0.5 mile more to Left Hand Grange Park. Here, the trail connects with the Niwot Loop Trail (see hike 22) and continues southwest toward Boulder. The park has a portable toilet and a picnic shelter. Follow the right path past a bench and across a wooden bridge, through trees and next to a small pond. The path turns slightly south to parallel Niwot Road. Cross Niwot Road at the marked crosswalk and end your hike at the Niwot Market shopping center. Take a break for refreshments before you walk or catch a ride back to the starting place in Longmont.

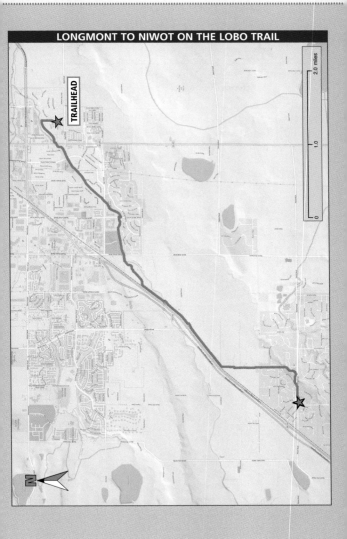

TRAILHEAD

2.0 miles

1.0

0

N

16. McIntosh Lake Loop and Agricultural Heritage Center

TRAILHEAD	McIntosh Lake
RATING	Easy
DISTANCE	3.5 miles, or 3.84 miles (with side trip to the Agricultural Heritage Center)
TIME	1.5 hours
ELEVATION GAIN	101 feet
USAGE	McIntosh Lake has both concrete and soft-surface multi-use trails that accommodate walkers/hikers and bicyclists. Dogs are allowed on leash.
STROLLER FRIENDLY	Yes

COMMENT: McIntosh Lake is one of Longmont's most popular recreational areas, offering an easy 3.5-mile loop trail that affords fantastic views of Longs Peak and Mt. Meeker.

Mt. Meeker and Longs Peak stands prominently in the distance west of McIntosh Lake.

"Dawson Silverwood," sculpture by Steve Jensen.

The lake is a reservoir that supplies local irrigation ditches, so it varies in water volume throughout the year. Named after George McIntosh, who homesteaded the area just north of the lake in 1868, the scenic natural area connects two city parks and the Boulder County Agricultural Heritage Center. Dawson Park, on the southeast side of the lake, has a playground, picnic shelter, and restrooms. Flanders Park, on the northeast side of the lake, offers the same amenities, with plenty of shade for picnics. Along the trail, a restroom is available on the far west side of the lake, and two port-a-potties are located adjacent to the parking area. The lake allows fishing and lightweight boating, and the Agricultural Heritage Center offers a fun and educational side trip, especially on summer weekends (see sidebar). Enjoy this family-friendly urban hike and make a day of it!

GETTING THERE: McIntosh Lake is located in northwest Longmont. The address of the parking lot at McIntosh Lake is 1905 Harvard Street. From Hover Street, head west on 17th Avenue and turn right onto Harvard. The parking lot is located next to a power substation. Parking is also available on Lakeshore Drive, southwest of Harvard, next to the Dawson Park playground. The park is a 15-minute walk from the nearest bus stop on Hover and 18th Avenue.

THE ROUTE: From the McIntosh Lake parking lot, turn left to hike clockwise around the lake. Pass Dawson Park (restrooms are available here) and stay to the right along the water. Look for the tall, silver treelike sculpture, "Dawson Silverwood," by Steve Jensen, near the water across from a picnic shelter, and step closer to read messages on the "fallen leaves" on the concrete pedestal. Continue walking west on the concrete path, enjoying the shade of the cottonwood trees. At about 0.75 mile, the path forks; continue straight ahead onto the crushed-gravel trail.

The soft-surface trail traverses an earthen dam for 0.5 mile on the southwest side of the lake. Notice the artful rusty iron distance markers at half-mile intervals around the lake. They are small and low to the ground, but fun to peek through for a new perspective on the path. As the trail curves to the northeast along the shore, you will see a few picnic tables in the shade of the trees and the red restroom structure ahead to the left. Follow the trail as it curves around a reedy wetland to the right along the lakeshore, with farmland on the left. At about the 2.0-mile mark, walk alongside the Agricultural Heritage Center fence to the signed trail that takes you north to the center. The center is only open on weekends in the warmer months and the first Saturday of each month through the winter, but an interpretive sign located at the trail turnoff provides interesting historical context for all passersby.

The Boulder County Agricultural Heritage Center makes an excellent side trip on summer weekends.

The Agricultural Heritage Center is open Friday through Sunday, 10 a.m. to 5 p.m. April through October, and the first Saturday of the month the rest of the year. It offers visitors a look into the life of Longmont's early farming and ranching families. Tour the 1909 farmhouse and nineteenth century barns, learn about local food production, check out the original smokehouse, and participate in free, family-friendly educational special events held twice a year. The land and buildings were sold to Boulder County by a grandson of George McIntosh in 1985, and the center opened in 2001 on what would have been McIntosh's 164th birthday. See bouldercounty.org for more details.

The Agricultural Heritage Center features a barn with interactive exhibits and places for kids to play and learn.

McIntosh Lake feeds the Oligarchy Ditch to irrigate nearby farms.

About 0.5 mile after the turnoff to the Agricultural Heritage Center, the crushed-gravel trail merges with a concrete path at a four-way junction with paths into the neighborhood on the left and into Flanders Park straight ahead. Take the path to the right along the water and walk in front of the park. Continue walking southeast around the lake for another 0.5 mile to return to the McIntosh Lake Trailhead and parking area.

TRAILHEAD

AGRICULTURAL HERITAGE CENTER

McIntosh Lake

0   0.1   0.2   0.3   0.4   0.5 miles

17. Open Sky Loop at Lagerman Agricultural Preserve

TRAILHEAD	Open Sky Loop
RATING	Easy
DISTANCE	5.0 miles
TIME	2 hours
ELEVATION GAIN	182 feet
USAGE	This wide, soft-surface trail is open to hikers, bicyclists, and equestrians. Be sure to walk on the right side of the trail and be aware of other trail users around you. Dogs are allowed on leash.
STROLLER FRIENDLY	Yes

COMMENT: The Open Sky Loop Trail encircles the northern portion of the Lagerman Agricultural Preserve. This land has been farmed since the late 1800s, when the Swedish congregation of a local Lutheran church purchased 160 acres as a "prastgard," or pastor's garden. The congregation farmed the land and gave the harvest to its pastor, Reverend Frederick Lagerman, as his salary. Lagerman Reservoir served as the

Early morning is the perfect time to take a hike on the Open Sky Loop.

The trail skirts and crosses several active ranches and farms.

irrigation reservoir for the farm. Today, the land is owned by Boulder County and is leased for agricultural use.

The 5.0-mile Open Sky Loop is true to its name; with little tree cover, it's a wonderful early morning, late-afternoon, or winter hike. Walking here provides a sense of what is known as "the right to roam" in the United Kingdom, where hikers can follow trails through private farms and properties,

provided they do not disturb livestock. The Open Sky Loop Trail rambles past tractor sheds and curious cows and offers overlooks onto pastoral farmland. It's also a fantastic place to sit and enjoy views of the Indian Peaks on a clear day. Restrooms and a picnic shelter are available at the trailhead, and Boulder County even provides a container of sunscreen in case hikers forget to bring their own.

GETTING THERE: The address of the parking lot for Lagerman Agricultural Preserve is 7100 Pike Road, Longmont. From the Diagonal Highway, go west on Niwot Road to North 73rd Street and turn right (north). Follow 73rd Street north as it curves around to the northeast and becomes North 75th Street. Turn left (west) onto Pike Road and follow the signs to the parking lot. The nearest bus connection is at the Diagonal Highway and Niwot Road Park and Ride. The BOLT bus runs between Longmont and Boulder.

The Open Sky Loop is aptly named: with wide-open views and little shade cover, this is a great hike for early morning, late evening, and winter.

Haystack Mountain is a prominent feature on the southwest horizon.

THE ROUTE: The well-marked Open Sky Loop Trail is easy to follow, because it's the only official trail north of Lagerman Reservoir. Follow the loop counterclockwise for the best views. From the Lagerman Agricultural Preserve parking lot, look for the Open Sky Loop Trail sign on the east side of the lot, just north (left) of the access road. The trail parallels the access road from Pike Road, then follows along the south side of Pike Road to just before 75th Street. The trail then crosses Pike Road and parallels 75th Street north for about 0.5 mile before curving to the northwest along the James Ditch.

The trail follows the ditch through an active farm. Follow the trail signs and be aware of any vehicles on the farm roads. You will pass an old tractor on the left and an active barn on the right, and then cross a small service road. The trail is well marked through the farm property. It continues north into a lush wetland, which is prime habitat for birds. Look for magpies, red-winged blackbirds, sparrows, finches, western meadowlarks, raptors, and more. As the trail turns to the west, it crosses the ditch and dips to the south through cow pastures.

The wide, multi-use trail accommodates all users comfortably.

Take care to follow the trail signs as you cross the farm access road at about the 2.0-mile mark, where the trail passes between two wooden fences just right of the access road and turns to the west beyond it. Be sure to stay on the crushed-gravel surface between the wooden fences. From here, enjoy great views to the left down into green pastures, with Haystack Mountain in the foreground and the Indian Peaks beyond.

Continue following the well-marked trail through the dry grassland at the westernmost extent of the loop. Turn south and walk past the farmhouses and barns on the property, enjoying the brief shade provided by cottonwood trees near an irrigation ditch. The trail jogs south over the ditch and briefly west before turning east toward 67th Street. Cross 67th Street and follow the trail back parallel along Pike Road to the parking area.

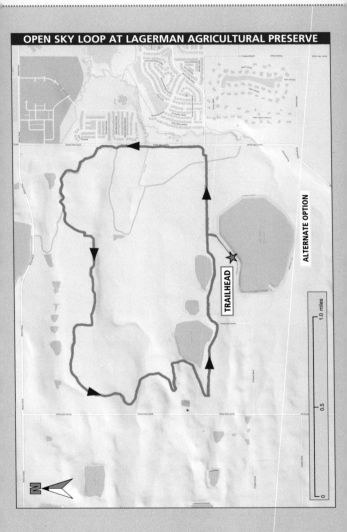

ALTERNATE OPTION

TRAILHEAD

1.0 miles

0.5

0

N

18. Pella Crossing Loops

TRAILHEAD	Pella Crossing
RATING	Easy
DISTANCE	3.3 miles
TIME	1.25 hours
ELEVATION GAIN	57 feet
USAGE	The Pella Crossing soft-surface multi-use trails are wide enough to easily accommodate hikers, dog walkers, bicyclists, and equestrians. Walk on the right and be aware of other trail users. Bicyclists are required to yield to walkers, and walkers must yield to horses.
STROLLER FRIENDLY	Yes

COMMENT: The tiny settlement of Hygiene was home to a tuberculosis sanitarium, the Hygiene House, in the 1880s. Today, Hygiene hosts a post office, a charming grocery store and deli, and a café and art gallery in what was once a service station. It's a delightful place to visit on your way to or from the Pella Crossing Trails, located just south of Hygiene Road.

Boulder County acquired the eastern side of the Pella Crossing property in 1992 and the western side in 1995. For generations, the land had been successively farmed and then mined for gravel used in road building. The former gravel pits now form several small reservoirs, and the area has become a lush wetland home to many species of birds and mammals. A group of Hygiene Elementary School fifth graders won a contest to name the property, calling it Pella Crossing because of its location between the two nineteenth century towns of Pella and North Pella. Today, groups of spandex-clad bicyclists ride down 75th Street, but it's easy to imagine stagecoaches rumbling through this distinctive

Looking west over Sunset Pond at Pella Crossing.

crossroads community surrounded by farmland. This is a fantastic place to walk with little ones, especially in the summer and fall, when the deciduous trees offer plenty of shade and spectacular color. Hike around one, two, or three of the ponds, bring binoculars to watch birds, or just relax under the trees for a quintessential Boulder County experience. Restrooms are available at the trailhead and at the western end of the park on the Marlatt Trails.

Picturesque Dragonfly Pond.

GETTING THERE: Pella Crossing sits just south of the junction of North 75th Street and Hygiene Road. From Longmont, take Highway 287 north to Highway 66, then go south on North 75th Street. From Boulder, take the Diagonal Highway north to Monarch Road, turn left, then take the next right onto North 71st Street, which becomes North 75th Street. The parking lot for Pella Crossing is on the east side of North 75th Street.

THE ROUTE: From the trailhead on the north side of the parking lot, walk straight ahead toward the first lake, Sunset Pond, and follow the trail to the left. Walk around the west side of Sunset Pond toward the junction with the trail leading west across 75th Street. This side of the lake is lined with cottonwood trees, and an old barn sits on the property. Turn left at the first trail junction, where the sign says "To Marlatt Trails," and walk to the crosswalk across 75th. Watch for cars and bicyclists. Cross the street and continue west on the Marlatt Trails (so named for the family who owned the property) to walk along the north side of Dragonfly Pond. All but one of the ponds at Pella Crossing allow fishing, and it is common to see anglers enjoying the sport on nice days.

Walk past the trail that goes between Dragonfly Pond and Poplar Pond, staying on the perimeter of the property. There is a wire fence on the right (north) side, and a horse ranch beyond. Along the water, you will see cattails, willows, and native grasses in this lush wetland habitat. Follow the trail around Poplar Pond as it curves to the south. There is a picnic table at about the 1.0-mile mark, situated underneath a giant cottonwood tree. Several irrigation ditches flow through this area, and as you continue on the trail around the southern end of Poplar Pond, notice the ditch on your right.

Take the right fork at the next trail junction over two ditches and into the trees. This is a delightful picnic area with tables and restrooms. Hike around the small clearing to Clearwater Pond and turn left. The dirt trail to the right dead-ends at private property. Head back around the small loop (there are several places to picnic here) to the trail between Poplar and Dragonfly Ponds. Walk along the earthen dam and stop to rest at any of the benches here. Once you reach the Marlatt

The wide, crushed-gravel trails at Pella Crossing are pleasant all year round.

Trails again at the north end of the ponds, turn right to head back toward 75th Street.

Cross 75th Street at the crosswalk and stay to the left. You will see a cluster of beehives on the right and train tracks on the left. Follow the train tracks along the northeast side of Sunset Pond to explore the full perimeter of the park and to get in the full mileage of this route. The trails around the eastern ponds at Pella Crossing offer less tree cover but broader views of the landscape. As you walk along the edge of Sunset Pond, look across the pond to the farmland beyond. Notice the bat box mounted high up on a pole on the left. As on the west side of the property, there is a trail between the two ponds on the east side, as well. Walk past that trail junction and continue along the train tracks toward Heron Lake.

Longs Peak is visible from the Marlatt Trails.

Cottonwood trees have long been considered sacred by indigenous peoples. This one looks as though it is reaching out to greet passersby!

Follow the trail along train tracks on the left and Heron Lake on the right. Just where the trail turns sharply to the south (right), there is a bench perfectly situated for looking southwest across the ponds to the mountains beyond. The trail heads south to the edge of the lake and then curves back around it to the west. At the southwest corner of the trail, stop to admire the giant cottonwood tree and the old silo beyond. On the south edge of Heron Lake, the cottonwood trees have wire cages around their trunks to prevent gnawing by beavers, who have already felled several trees along the lake edge. From here, you can look across Heron Lake to see Longs Peak to the west.

The trail turns north between Webster Pond on the left (the only pond where fishing is not allowed) and Sunset Pond. Follow either of the trails back toward the picnic shelter and the parking lot beyond.

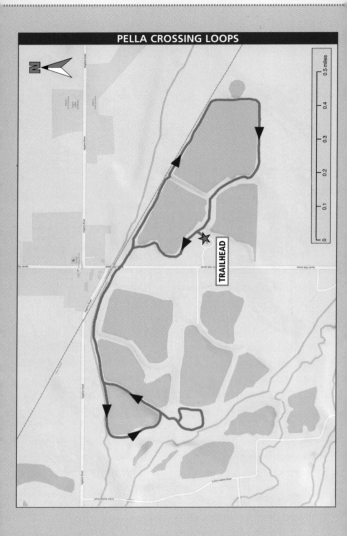

PELLA CROSSING LOOPS

TRAILHEAD

0   0.1   0.2   0.3   0.4   0.5 miles

19. St. Vrain Greenway Stroll

TRAILHEAD	Golden Ponds Park
RATING	Easy
DISTANCE	4.3 miles (out and back)
TIME	1.5–2 hours
ELEVATION GAIN	46 feet
USAGE	The St. Vrain Greenway is a mix of concrete and soft-surface multi-use trails. It is open to walkers/hikers and bicyclists. Dogs are allowed on leash.
STROLLER FRIENDLY	Yes

COMMENT: The St. Vrain Creek runs from the mountains west of Lyons through Longmont and joins the South Platte River in adjacent Weld County. In September 2013, massive flash flooding devastated the town of Lyons and much of Longmont as three times the St. Vrain channel's maximum capacity of water ripped apart the banks of the creek and

The view from Golden Ponds, looking west.

Golden Ponds was named for Vernon Golden, depicted in this statue.

inundated surrounding areas. The flooding destroyed the then-existing St. Vrain Greenway, a path and trail system connecting Golden Ponds Park in the west with Sandstone Ranch in the east. Over the past six years, the City of Longmont has invested in restoring the greenway and improving the creek channel to provide greater resiliency in future floods. The city also has an extensive Art in Public Places collection, and several sculptures add visual interest and information along the corridor. Urban hikers and families will soon be able to explore the full 8.0-mile stretch of the St. Vrain Greenway, enjoy more nature play and water recreation opportunities along the way, and walk the width of Longmont. For now, enjoy shorter sections of the greenway as they open to the public, including this three-loop route on the west end of the system that includes the Boulder County Farmer's Market, a perfect place to stop on a Saturday morning. Restrooms are available at Golden Ponds Park, Rogers Grove Park, and Izaak Walton Park.

GETTING THERE: The address of Golden Ponds Park is 2651 3rd Avenue, Longmont. The parking area is just west of Hover Street on 3rd Avenue. From Main Street (Highway 287), go west on 9th to Hover and turn south, cross the train tracks, and immediately turn right on 3rd. From the Diagonal Highway, turn left (north) on Hover, drive past Rogers Grove Park on the right, and turn left onto 3rd immediately after crossing St. Vrain Creek. The entrance to the park is disguised by two self-storage companies; keep driving west to the parking area. The park is also accessible by the BOLT, J, and LD2 buses, all of which stop right at Hover and 3rd Avenue.

THE ROUTE: From the Golden Ponds parking lot, walk west on the concrete path past the restrooms on the right and two picnic shelters on the left. As the concrete path turns to the left between the first two ponds, notice the bronze sculpture, "Golden Days," at the junction on the right. The sculpture depicts Vernon Golden, whose family donated the land for the park to the City of Longmont. Like many ponds in Boulder County, the reservoirs at Golden Ponds are old gravel quarries that filled with water after excavation activity stopped.

Strolling along the St. Vrain provides a relaxing experience.

Vernon Golden had quarried gravel on the site, and wanted the land restored to nature for recreational enjoyment.

To explore the full perimeter of Golden Ponds, keep walking west past the sculpture onto the soft-surface trail. Follow the trail northwest along the northern edge of the two ponds. There is a small picnic shelter at the next trail junction, where a path extends to the southwest between the two ponds. Continue walking west all the way around the westernmost pond. Stop to take in the spectacular views of Longs Peak beyond the fence between the trail and another pond to the west, which is not part of the park. The trail bends to the southeast around the pond. Follow it along the southern edge of the ponds, through a beautiful cottonwood-lined corridor. Rejoin the concrete path and turn right at the spillway, a small "waterfall" creating a drop in the St. Vrain Creek channel. Continue over a wooden footbridge in front of the spillway. There are restrooms and a few picnic shelters at the path junction here.

Turn left to follow the concrete path alongside the creek, heading east. Alternatively, you can cross Lykins Gulch (the body of water straight ahead) by walking on the large stepping

Flowers and mountain views on the St. Vrain Greenway.

"Golden Ponds Guardian," sculpture by Steven Carmer.

stones visible from the path. The stepping stones are typically exposed when the water level is low, and they are fun to cross in late summer, when the cattails and native grasses are high, creating an enchanting corridor down to the water. If you take the stepping stones, turn left around the lake to rejoin the concrete path heading east. Look for the bronze sculpture of a frog on a block of sandstone at the junction with the Lykins Gulch Trail. There is also a picnic shelter here. Continue walking east on the path along the creek and follow the path to the left to take the Hover Street underpass.

On the east side of Hover, choose either the dirt path to the left along the water or stay on the concrete path to walk alongside Rogers Grove Park. There are benches under the trees by the creek, making that path a good choice on warmer days. Continue walking east around the edge of the park. As the path bends to the south, notice the amphitheater-style seating in the park on the right, as well as the restroom pavilion. Take a break here, if needed, or continue walking south along the path. At the junction with the soft-surface path, turn right to go around the western edge of the pond at the

Stop by the Longmont Farmers Market on Saturday mornings, on the path to the Boulder County Fairgrounds.

Boulder County Fairgrounds. This is a lovely natural area, and the path leads to the site of the Boulder County Farmer's Market, which happens every Saturday from 8 a.m. to 1 p.m, April through November. Stop by for delicious local food, live music, and kids' activities.

Continue walking around the pond and follow the concrete path from the Farmer's Market site north to rejoin the greenway. Cross the wooden bridge over the St. Vrain Creek and turn right. Here, again, you can choose to remain on the concrete path or take a narrow dirt trail along the water. Several "Details of Nature" sculptures by Robert Tully line the concrete path. Walk east along the path and take the underpass under South Sunset Street. Izaak Walton Park is just east of Sunset. This park has a clubhouse and event space, picnic shelters, restrooms, and a kids' fishing pond. Posted signage notes that only people under age 15 are allowed to fish in the pond (with parents' help), and the park hosts a youth fishing program (see longmontcolorado.gov for information).

Stop to take a break and enjoy the park before turning around, or walk a short way farther east to Boston Avenue,

Stroll across the stepping stones at Lykins Gulch in the summer.

where you can stop at Left Hand Brewing, a local microbrewery, for refreshments. When you're ready, head back west along the greenway path. At the junction with the path to the Boulder County Fairgrounds, stay to the right to continue straight on to Rogers Grove Park. Notice another of Robert Tully's sculptures here, "Listening Stones." The city's Art in Public Places program commissioned many works of art placed along the greenway in the late 1990s and early 2000s before the flood. "Listening Stones" features a parabolic sound mirror carved into the center stone, which used to reflect the sounds of the creek to listeners sitting in front of it. After the 2013 flood, the creek channel moved to the north, too far from the stone to work as intended. The city may move the artwork as part of the greenway restoration program.

Take the Hover Street underpass and continue west to Golden Ponds Park. Stay on the concrete path between the first and second ponds to reach the parking area more quickly, or follow the crushed-gravel path around the perimeter again for a longer hike.

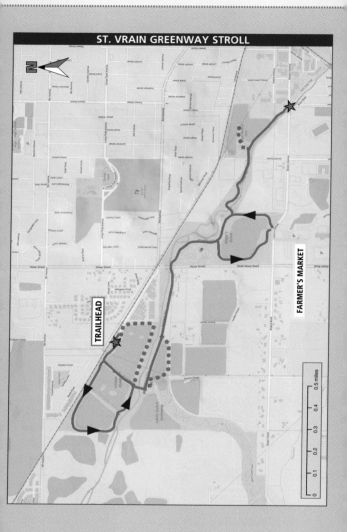

TRAILHEAD

FARMER'S MARKET

| 0 | 0.1 | 0.2 | 0.3 | 0.4 | 0.5 miles |

20. Harper Lake and Davidson Mesa Figure 8

TRAILHEAD	Harper Lake
RATING	Easy
DISTANCE	4.27 miles
TIME	1.5 hours
ELEVATION GAIN	82 feet
USAGE	Both soft-surface trails allow bicyclists, so be sure to walk on the right side of the trail and be aware of trail users around you. Bike activity is greatest on weekends. Dogs are allowed on Davidson Mesa Open Space, and there is an enclosed off-leash area at the trailhead on the west side of McCaslin Boulevard. Dogs are not allowed at Harper Lake.
STROLLER FRIENDLY	Yes

COMMENT: For spectacular views of Longs Peak and the Front Range, you can't beat Davidson Mesa Open Space. This figure-8 route offers plenty of places to sit and admire

Harper Lake is an oasis of calm in Louisville.

The Harper Lake and Davidson Mesa trailheads feature polished sculptural rocks where hikers can pause and enjoy the scenery.

the vista. The wide, packed-gravel and dirt trails around Harper Lake and Davidson Mesa Open Space wind through native grassland, where black-tailed prairie dogs play and Western meadowlarks sing. Admire the abundant yucca growing on the mesa and enjoy geese and ducks on the lake. Please note that dogs are only allowed on the Davidson Mesa side (west of McCaslin Boulevard) and are not allowed at any time around Harper Lake, as the lake supplies water for the City of Louisville. Be sure to wear or bring sun protection on this hike; it's out in the open all the way, at 5,690 feet above sea level. This is a great choice for an energizing winter hike. Restrooms are available at the Harper Lake Trailhead.

GETTING THERE: The Harper Lake Trailhead is located just east of McCaslin Boulevard at Washington Avenue in Louisville. From McCaslin, turn onto Washington Ave. and pull into the parking lot on the north side of the street. Parking is also available across McCaslin at the Davidson Mesa Open Space Trailhead. The nearest bus stop is at South Boulder Road and McCaslin Boulevard, approximately 0.5 mile north of Harper Lake. Take the DASH bus down South Boulder Road to get there, then walk south along the Leon Wurl Wildlife Sanctuary connector trail to Harper Lake.

THE ROUTE: Starting at the Harper Lake parking lot off Washington Avenue, take a right from the trailhead sign to walk along the southeast side of the lake. The soft-surface trail is comfortably wide enough for both walkers and bicyclists, and it branches into two parallel trails for a while at the first large cottonwood tree. Stop and admire the view from the bench by the tree, or keep going along the lakeshore (watch out for nesting Canada geese in the spring, which can be very territorial!). Follow the path's curve to the north and cross a small bridge. Continue around the lake to the northwest. This area is designated as the Leon Wurl Wildlife Sanctuary, named for a former City of Louisville administrator. Another bench is available on west side of the lake, next to a rock with a plaque commemorating the "valiant cowboy" for whom the area is named.

In just under 1.0 mile, you will arrive back at the Harper Lake Trailhead. Turn right and walk on the pavement

Looking west over Harper Lake.

through the McCaslin Boulevard underpass. On the other side, follow the pavement past the enclosed off-leash dog area to the Davidson Mesa Open Space Trailhead (look for a map kiosk and a couple of stone benches on the south side of the parking lot). Walk left past the trail map kiosk onto the packed-gravel trail, heading southwest. Stick to the perimeter of the mesa for the full mileage of this figure-8 hike. Follow the trail along a ditch bordered by a few cottonwood trees, heading toward a red-brick office building in the development on the left. Near the office building is a trail that bisects the oval Davidson Mesa perimeter trail; stay to the left unless you want to cut your hike short and return early via the trail to the right.

As you walk through the natural grassland on the mesa, look for black-tailed prairie dogs popping in and out of their burrows near the trail. In the fall and spring, listen for western meadowlarks and red-winged blackbirds, and watch

Davidson Mesa is a broad native grassland, lush and green in the spring and golden in the late summer and fall.

Sandstone benches are available around the Davidson Mesa trails.

for stealthy red-tailed hawks who swoop over the grassland looking for prey. Native red sandstone benches are available for resting and enjoying the wildlife and mountain views about every 0.25 mile.

Continue walking southwest along the trail under the large electrical transmission lines. The best mountain views are on the west side of the wires, after about mile 2.0. At the 2.0-mile mark, you will reach an entrance to the trail from the US 36 Bikeway, a "highway for cyclists" between Boulder and Denver completed in 2017. Stay on the dirt trail, which curves around to the north at this point. Walk alongside the fences separating the neighboring houses from the trail. Keep to the perimeter, always taking the left trail at the forks. As the trail cuts back around to the east after the houses, stop at the bench engraved, "Peace, Love and Joyful Reflection," to gaze over the yucca plants at Longs Peak. It's a spectacular view.

Head back along the trail to the northeast to the Davidson Mesa Trailhead, then follow the pavement back through the Harper Lake underpass and the parking lot.

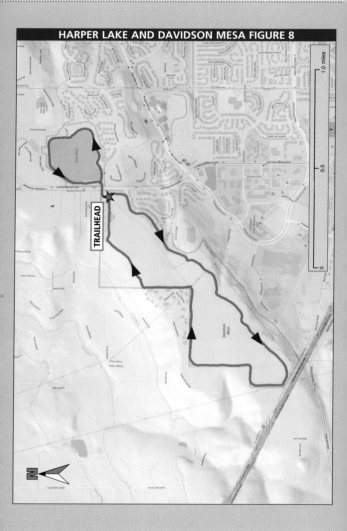

TRAILHEAD

1.0 miles

0.5

0

N

21. North Open Space Lollipop

TRAILHEAD	Annette Brand Park
RATING	Easy
DISTANCE	4.2 miles
TIME	2 hours or more, with time to play
ELEVATION GAIN	220 feet
USAGE	This concrete-surface multi-use path is open to bicyclists and walkers. Dogs are allowed. Walk on the right side of the path and be aware of other path users around you, knowing that bicyclists may approach from behind. Bicyclists must yield to walkers, but especially when walking with little ones, help everyone in your group travel on the right.
STROLLER FRIENDLY	Yes

COMMENT: Spend the day outdoors with the little people in your life! This lollipop-shaped route invites you to play your way through Louisville's North Open Space. Along the way, you'll find lots of fun places to explore, including two

Louisville's North Open Space offers miles of beautiful trails.

parks with play structures and an enchanting cottonwood forest, with child-sized log structures perfect for growing imaginations. This urban hike is ideal for families using strollers and accompanying little ones just learning how to ride a bike, or for anyone who wants to get a few miles in and explore the City of Louisville's extensive multi-use path network. Whether you live in the area or are just visiting, this urban hike will top your list for child-friendly destinations with just the right balance of wild nature and urban amenities. Note that restrooms are not readily available along this route, but there is a portable toilet at Centennial Park.

GETTING THERE: Annette Brand Park is located at 961 Azure Way. From South Boulder Road, turn north onto Continental View Drive (at the McCaslin Boulevard stoplight) and follow Continental View Drive north, which turns into Azure Way as the street turns east. Azure Way ends at West Plum Circle, and the park sits at the junction of the two streets. Park along the street. You can also approach the park from Hays Drive off of South Boulder Road. The nearest bus stop is on South Boulder Road just east of Hays Drive. The DASH bus travels both directions on South Boulder Road, from downtown Boulder to downtown Lafayette through Louisville. If you take the bus, walk north on Hays Drive to the path leading into the park just past West Barberry Court.

THE ROUTE: Starting at the north end of Annette Brand Park, walk along the concrete path that winds past the playground and the picnic shelter, both of which are bordered by mature evergreen trees. The playground at Annette Brand offers both a toddler-sized play structure and one for older children, with plenty of well-shaded benches and picnic tables surrounding the play area. Follow the path around to the south and take a left at the first junction to head due east (the path that continues along the park terminates at South Boulder Road).

Stop to explore the stick structures in the woods near Keith Helart Park.

Walking east, you will notice a chain-link fence on your left. The fence surrounds Louisville Reservoir and the city's water treatment plant. Continue straight along the fence, under the tall electrical tower, and walk past the entrance to the water treatment plant following the concrete path. Half a mile in, the path turns north with switchbacks down the hill. The bench at the top of the hill is a good place to stop and make sure any little ones walking with you are strapped in before you head down the steep slope. The switchbacks make the path easily navigable with a stroller, but the path is likely too steep for a young child on a bike (though older children may love the ride!).

As the path turns back east, it affords a wonderful view of the North Open Space. You will see a cottonwood and oak forest to the right, the water treatment plant property to the left, and broad native grasslands straight ahead. In the summer and fall, the forest is ablaze with color. In the winter and early spring, look for exposed nests high in the tree branches. Listen for blue jays and other native birds as you walk through the open space.

The concrete path continues northeast toward the cottonwood trees and the two parallel irrigation ditches they line: the Highline Lateral Ditch and the Goodhue Ditch. The wooden bridge over the second ditch ends at a T-shaped path intersection, and at the top of the T, spot the forest where a few stick structures have been built by local families. The houses and lean-tos are great fun to explore with children; follow the social trail into the forest and have a look around or take the left (north) fork to continue walking toward Keith Helart Park. The park offers a toddler-friendly play structure and a pleasantly shaded picnic shelter, as well as additional benches around the play structure. It's a great place to take a lunch break or a rest.

From Keith Helart Park, follow the concrete path northeast into the Callahan Open Space; look for the trail sign on the north side of the park. The path takes you through a meadow, with houses fenced off to the right. This is a great place to catch a glimpse of Longs Peak through the trees on the left, and it's also the ideal location to let a new bicyclist try out his or her wheels. Follow the path to a triangular intersection. You will see railroad tracks running north-south from here. Freight trains travel along these tracks regularly, which is another great attraction for young children. Turn right and follow the tracks to the southeast. The wide, open path travels alongside a neighborhood with lots of trees, lush gardens, local artwork, and

Look for acorns on the oak trees along the path in the fall.

The Boulder Ramblers on the North Open Space Trail.

other oddities ideal for playing "I Spy." Stay to the left, taking the path to its terminus at Centennial Drive.

Once you reach Centennial Drive, the path curves back around to the southwest along the Highline Lateral Ditch. Use the crosswalk to cross Centennial. If you and your walking companions need a break or a snack, walk south on Centennial to the shopping center at the corner of Centennial and South Boulder Road, where plenty of options for refreshments are available. Otherwise, follow the concrete path along the ditch.

The path ends at Garfield Avenue, just east of Centennial Park. Turn right on Garfield and head north to the intersection of Garfield and Centennial Drive, 0.3 mile ahead. Turn left onto Centennial and walk to the path entrance to the North Open Space, just 0.1 mile farther. Cross the street and rejoin the North Open Space path. This branch of the path connects back to Keith Helart Park and the wooden bridge by the play forest. Follow the path to the wooden bridge to complete the lollipop circle.

Turn left to cross the wooden bridge and take the path back west along the "stick" of the lollipop. It is just over 1.0 mile to Annette Brand Park from here, up the hill to the water treatment plant and back along the fence.

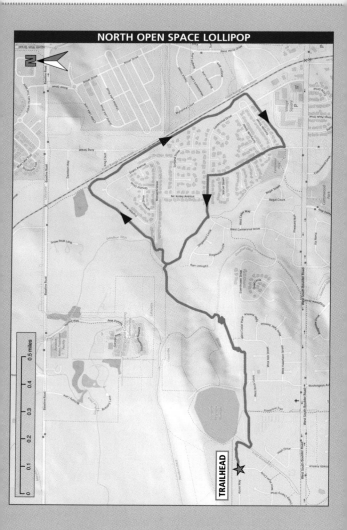

TRAILHEAD

22. Niwot Loop Adventure

TRAILHEAD	Niwot Loop
RATING	Moderate
DISTANCE	6.4 miles
TIME	3 hours
ELEVATION GAIN	314 feet
USAGE	The Niwot Loop Trails are soft-surface multi-use trails open to hikers, bicyclists, and equestrians. Dogs are allowed on leash.
STROLLER FRIENDLY	Yes

COMMENT: The town of Niwot is named after Chief Niwot, or Left Hand, a nineteenth-century leader of the Southern Arapaho people native to the Boulder area. He is commemorated around Boulder County in art and sculpture, including many painted left-hand statues placed around central Niwot. The six trails that comprise the Niwot Loop were built over the past 15 years in tandem with subdivision development in the area and as part of Boulder County's Longmont-to-Boulder (LoBo) Regional Trail Project. They offer hikers fantastic

The Niwot Loop Trails take hikers through forests and open grasslands.

Looking west from the Legend Ridge Open Space on the Niwot Loop.

views of the Front Range while winding through agricultural areas and alongside irrigation ditches, natural wetlands, and neighborhoods. The route described here follows the perimeter of the Niwot Loop system. Explore the area further by following the trail map provided at bouldercounty.org/open-space/parks-and-trails. A portable toilet is available at the Lefthand Valley Grange Trailhead at North 83rd Street and Niwot Road, but no other facilities are provided along this route. Be sure to carry plenty of water, and wear sunscreen and sun protection when you hit the trail.

GETTING THERE: This route begins at the Niwot Loop Trailhead on North 79th Street just north of Mineral Road. From Longmont or Boulder, take the Diagonal Highway to Mineral Road (Highway 52) and go east to North 79th Street. Turn left (north); the trailhead will be on your right.

THE ROUTE: From the Niwot Loop Trailhead, start at the wooden bridge on the north side of the parking lot. Cross that bridge over the Boulder and Left Hand Ditch, then cross another wooden bridge over the Boulder and Whiterock

Ditch. Just past the second bridge, notice the Niwot Trails sign, and follow the arrow to the right to start on the Somerset Trail. The Somerset Trail leads east past a prairie dog town on the right and a neighborhood on the left. At about 0.75 mile, stay to the right at the junction, continuing on the Somerset Trail, and notice the interpretive sign about the geology of the area. Look for the unusual "turtleback" sandstone formations on the ground.

Continue around a small pond. The trail stops at Somerset Drive; cross the street and continue walking on the trail to the east. This is the southern edge of the Legend Ridge Loop Trail around the subdivision of that name. Follow the Legend Ridge Loop around to the north. At just over 2.0 miles, you will reach the junction with the Niwot Hills Trail. Turn right here after taking a moment to enjoy the stunning mountain view at this intersection. The Niwot Hills Trail, which is a gray crushed-gravel trail, heads north and crosses the access road to the Left Hand Water District and an access road to the houses on the right a little farther. Keep going north until you reach the crosswalk at Niwot Road. Cross the road and turn right to walk alongside a wooden fence. Go to the end of that section of fence and turn left onto the Cougar Trail

Scenic farms surround the Niwot Loop Trails.

(named for the mascot of nearby Niwot High School). Stay on the Cougar Trail and walk to the left, past two entrances to the Niwot High School athletic fields. The trail takes you alongside the Boulder and Whiterock Ditch.

At about 3.1 miles, turn right at the next junction onto the Overbrook Trail. This trail takes you north for about 0.3 mile, then turns due west. As the trail heads west and then southwest, it follows Dry Creek, the natural waterway where gold was discovered in 1858. The southwest section of the Overbrook Trail is a lush marshland with abundant cattails and cottonwoods. At about 4.25 miles, cross North 83rd Street at the crosswalk. Here, you will join the Longmont-to-Boulder (LoBo) Trail. The Lefthand Valley Grange Trailhead is to your left, and a portable toilet and picnic shelter are available there. Follow the trail sign pointing to Boulder and take the soft-surface trail to the concrete section that leads to the Niwot Road underpass. Pass an area with two benches and a wooden bridge on your right, and continue to the left to enter the underpass. Enjoy looking at the historical art murals inside the underpass!

On the south side of the underpass, walk toward the soft-surface trail straight ahead. Rejoin the packed-gravel LoBo Trail and walk alongside Dry Creek to the southwest. At the

Enjoy views of the mountains as you hike west toward Niwot.

The Niwot Loop connects with the LoBo Trail and links several neighborhoods.

5.0-mile mark, walk past a small wooden bridge over the creek to your right and notice the social trails into the neighborhoods in the area. Continue to the right on the LoBo Trail. Take the crosswalk across North 79th Street. At the next trail junction, you will see a bench and a pond. Stay to the left and continue walking toward Monarch Road. At Monarch Road, take the crosswalk and walk past the small Monarch Park Trailhead on the right. Here, the LoBo Trail turns almost due south and takes you through an active agricultural area. Looking straight ahead, you can see Green Mountain and the Flatirons to the south. Go through the gates at either end of the farm on this section of the trail.

Follow the LoBo Trail, look for the sign that points to Boulder, and cross the wooden bridge over Dry Creek going to the left. At about 6.0 miles, the LoBo Trail turns to the right toward Boulder; stay to the left and walk toward the traffic light in the distance at North 79th and Mineral Road. At this point, you will walk parallel to Mineral Road alongside a prairie dog colony. Go through the gate at 79th Street, cross at the crosswalk, and return to the parking lot.

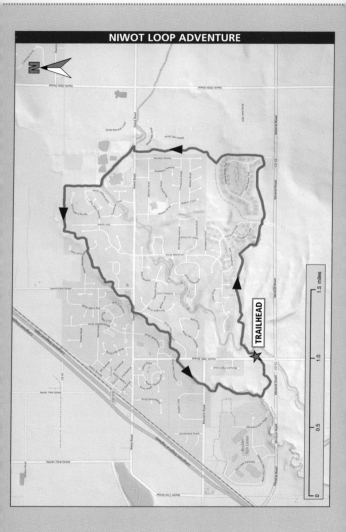

TRAILHEAD

About the Author

Darcy Kitching designs and leads urban hikes and community engagement walks with the Walk-2Connect Cooperative, the Boulder Ramblers, and the City of Boulder. Darcy grew up in suburban Denver, traveled to all 50 states, and explored six continents throughout her young adulthood, then settled in south Boulder with her scientist husband. Together, they hike and travel regularly, and they have a young son who also loves to play outdoors. A lifelong writer and passionate cross-sectoral thinker, Darcy has contributed to a wide variety of publications, from the specialty coffee trade magazine *Fresh Cup* to the United Nations' *State of the World Cities Report*. Darcy proudly defies boundaries, mobilizing her varied background in writing, early childhood education, and urban planning to consult on child-friendly cities, creative community engagement strategies, urban walkability, and community development. She believes walking is the best way to get to know a place, and she loves helping people discover the hidden beauty and natural wonder of cities. Darcy is also a trained Boulder County volunteer naturalist and a skilled photographer.

Photo by Cliff Grassmick for the *Boulder Daily Camera*, 6/30/2018

Illustration by Jesse Crock

Join Today.
Adventure Tomorrow.

The Colorado Mountain Club helps you maximize living in an outdoor playground and connects you with other adventure-loving mountaineers. We summit 14ers, climb rock faces, work to protect the mountain experience, and educate generations of Coloradans.

www.cmc.org